MY ANCESTC
IRISH

by Alan Stewart

SOCIETY OF GENEALOGISTS ENTERPRISES LTD.

Published by
Society of Genealogists Enterprises Limited
14 Charterhouse Buildings, Goswell Road
London EC1M 7BA.

© Alan Stewart and Society of Genealogists 2012.

ISBN: 978-1-907199-14-1

British Library Cataloguing in Publication Data.
A CIP Catalogue record for this book is available from the British Library.

The Society of Genealogists Enterprises Limited is a wholly owned
subsidiary of the Society of Genealogists, a registered charity, no 233701.

About the Author

Alan Stewart is a former information technology manager who has been tracing his own ancestors for over 30 years. During all of this time he has been a member of the Society of Genealogists (SoG). Alan has been published in the *Financial Times* and *Encyclopedia Britannica*, writes for several family history magazines (both in the United Kingdom and in North America), gives talks at the SoG library in London, and is a member of the User Group for the ScotlandsPeople website. This is Alan's fifth published book, and his fourth on family history.

Cover Images - Foreground: *Irish Colleen* , by 'Snapshots of the Past', 2007. Background: *Historic Irish Cemetery* by Dave Grey, 2008. Watermark: Celtic knot. Creative Commons licences.

CONTENTS

List of illustrations

CHAPTER ONE
Introduction to Irish Records

S ince family history has become an increasingly popular pastime for many people with roots in Ireland, I felt there was a need for a concise and straightforward guide to help all those starting to trace their Irish ancestry. This book is intended not only for Irishmen and women but also for those outside Ireland with knowledge, perhaps of tracing English and Welsh families, but seeking guidance about the differences and challenges of Irish research.

You may have heard that researching your ancestors in Ireland is more challenging than in many other countries, as a fire at the Public Record Office of Ireland (PROI) in 1922 caused the loss of many Irish records. These included the 1821-1851 censuses (the 1861-1891 censuses had already been destroyed by British Government order), wills proved before about 1900, and about 60% of the Church of Ireland (Protestant) parish registers.

All is not lost, however, and family historians can trace their ancestors in Ireland, as many indexes, transcriptions and original images of the Irish records do still exist (including civil registration births, marriages and deaths; the 1901 and 1911 censuses; various census substitutes; Roman Catholic parish registers; the remaining Church of Ireland parish registers; many wills proved from 1858 onwards; and United Kingdom armed forces records) and many have been made available online.

So much so, that it's now possible to do much of your basic Irish research without ever having to set foot in Ireland. Of course, I'm not saying you shouldn't visit Ireland - only that you may not have to do so to find your Irish ancestors.

Up to the end of December 1921, all of Ireland formed part of the United Kingdom, but on 1 January 1922, the island was partitioned. The six counties in the north-east became known as Northern Ireland (which is still part of the UK) and the remaining 26 counties became the Irish Free State, known as Eire from 1937 and the Republic of Ireland since 1949.

Civil registration

Civil birth, marriage and death records were not affected by the 1922 fire. Civil registration of non-Roman Catholic marriages began in Ireland on 1 April 1845, and of births, deaths and Catholic marriages on 1 January 1864. The information on Irish civil registration records is very similar to that on English and Welsh records. Chapter 2 explains how the Irish system works.

Census returns

The first official census in Ireland was held in 1821, but unfortunately, the 1901 and 1911 are the only complete Irish censuses surviving and open to the public. A number of fragments and abstracts of parts of the 1821-1871 censuses have survived and these are described in Chapter 3.

Census substitutes

Because of the loss of the 19th century censuses, the land valuations that list heads of households have taken on a greater significance than they would have otherwise. The most important of these are Griffith's Valuation carried out between 1847 and 1864, and the Tithe Applotment Books which were compiled between 1823 and 1837. I've covered these and other lists in Chapter 4.

Church registers

Until the end of 1870, the Church of Ireland (an Anglican church) was the established church in the country, although Roman Catholicism was the denomination of the majority of the population. Due to an influx of migrants from Scotland in the 17th century, there are many Presbyterians in Ulster.

Although only Church of Ireland registers were destroyed in 1922, most Roman Catholic and Presbyterian registers don't begin until the mid-19th century. There are almost no surviving Church of Ireland bishops' transcripts. In Chapter 5, I've explained the location and use of church records.

Wills and administrations

Up to 1858, Irish wills (like those of England and Wales) were proved in church courts, the most important of which was the Prerogative Court of the Archbishop of Armagh (the equivalent of the Prerogative Court of Canterbury for England and Wales). Below that court were the diocesan (or consistory) courts of the Church of Ireland bishops and two 'peculiar' courts not subject to a bishop's authority. Most of the wills proved in the church courts were destroyed in 1922.

As in England and Wales, district civil probate registries were established in 1858, with a Principal Probate Registry in Dublin. Although the original wills proved in the district registries up to 1899 were destroyed, copies that had been made are still in existence. Unfortunately, those proved at the Principal Probate Registry up to 1904 had not been copied and were therefore lost in 1922.

Nevertheless, indexes to wills were made (as well as copies and abstracts), before the original wills were destroyed, and this may enable you to find some probate documents and evidence. Wills and administrations are described in Chapter 6.

Online records

In recent years, images or transcriptions of many Irish records have been made available online free of charge, including those of the 1901 and 1911 censuses at **www.census.nationalarchives.ie** and Griffith's Valuation at the Ask About Ireland website **www.askaboutireland.ie/griffith-valuation/index.xml**.

You can search the civil registration indexes up to 1958 for the Irish Free State/Republic (and for all of Ireland before 1922) at FamilySearch **www.familysearch.org** and also at Ancestry.co.uk **www.ancestry.co.uk**.

In addition, the Irish Family History Foundation has set up the Roots Ireland website **www.rootsireland.ie**, which currently holds transcriptions of more than 19 million records. Most of these (over 14 million) are birth, marriage and death records from both church registers and the civil registration. Most of the counties and parts of counties not covered by Roots Ireland are on the rival Irish Genealogy site **www.irishgenealogy.ie**.

Although most Irish wills were destroyed in 1922, you can search an index of surviving abstracts, extracts and copies of pre-1858 Irish wills at the Irish Origins website **www.irishorigins.com** and at Findmypast Ireland **www.findmypast.ie**. A similar index for what is now Northern Ireland has been made available online by the Public Record Office of Northern Ireland (PRONI) **www.proni.gov.uk**.

A number of will indexes had been compiled before 1922, and Ancestry.co.uk has indexes of the wills proved in the Prerogative Court of the Archbishop of Armagh and in many of the local diocesan courts, as well as abstracts of some 18th century wills. In most cases, these wills no longer exist.

These and other useful online resources are covered in Chapter 14.

Irish local government

Over the centuries, Ireland had been divided into 32 counties for administrative purposes, and all references in this book will be to the historic counties.

The county system continued after partition in 1922, although in the Irish Free State King's and Queen's Counties were renamed Offaly and Laois (or Leix). The Republic of Ireland still uses counties, but Northern Ireland's six counties were divided into 26 districts in 1973, one of which was the former county of Fermanagh.

In 1994, County Dublin in the Republic of Ireland was divided into Dublin City and the counties of Dun Laoghaire-Rathdown, Fingal and South Dublin. Cork, Galway, Limerick and Waterford are also city councils in the Republic of Ireland.

Below county level, Ireland was divided into baronies, which were similar to hundreds and wapentakes in England. These consisted, in turn, of many parishes, which were further divided into 'townlands' (an ancient land division, which ranged in size from less than one acre to more than 7,000 acres, although most were about 200-400 acres in size).

Civil parishes covered roughly the same area as those of the Church of Ireland, but Roman Catholic parishes were larger and often had different names. Chapter 7 looks at records of land and property, while Chapter 9 shows some very useful map resources that may help your research.

Many Irishmen served in the armed forces and may be found in the resources covered by Chapter 8, while Irish newspapers are extremely useful and their use is described in Chapter 10. I've outlined naming patterns, surnames and the clan system, a significant feature of Irish history and genealogy, in Chapter 11, together with immigration and emigration.

The various statistical surveys and histories described in Chapter 12 will provide good local insight for your Irish research, while the surviving monumental inscriptions listed in Chapter 13 are an underused resource. A guide to the many excellent archives, libraries and family history societies in Ireland can be found in Chapters 16 and 17, along with a select bibliography of useful reading matter to take your Irish family history further.

The library of the Society of Genealogists

At the end of several chapters of this book, I've indicated that there are record copies or transcriptions in the library of the Society of Genealogists in central London. In addition, Chapter 15 lists many other Irish resources in the library.

The townland of Ballymagrorty Irish, looking to the sea, 2008, by Louise Price.

CHAPTER TWO
Civil Registration

In Ireland, civil registration of non-Roman Catholic marriages began on 1 April 1845, with births, deaths and Catholic marriages following on 1 January 1864. At that time, the whole island, which was part of the United Kingdom of Great Britain and Ireland, had a single registration system.

After a war of independence (the Anglo-Irish War) from January 1919 until July 1921, the island was divided in two. On 1 January 1922, the larger part (26 of the 32 Irish counties) became a dominion within the British Empire (later the Commonwealth), in a similar way to Australia, Canada and New Zealand. It was known as the Irish Free State and had Dublin as its capital.

In 1937, the Free State became a republic under the name of Eire (in Irish) or Ireland (in English), leaving the Commonwealth in 1948 to become the Republic of Ireland the following year.

In 1921, the remaining six Irish counties (Antrim, Armagh, Down, Fermanagh, Derry/Londonderry and Tyrone) had become Northern Ireland, with Belfast as its capital. Northern Ireland remains part of the United Kingdom. The Irish Free State/Republic and Northern Ireland have had separate civil registration systems since that time.

7

The Irish Republic's General Register Office (GRO) holds birth, marriage and death records for the whole island up to the end of 1921, as well as those for the Irish Free State/Republic from the beginning of 1922. The GRO moved its headquarters from Dublin to Roscommon in 2005, but continues to have a research room in Dublin.

The General Register Office of Northern Ireland (GRONI) in Belfast holds birth and death registrations from 1864 onwards for what is now Northern Ireland, as well as marriage registrations for the area from 1922 onwards. Pre-1922 marriage records for the area are held by district registrars in Northern Ireland (and by the GRO in Dublin).

You can find a map of the civil registration districts of Ireland at **www.connorsgenealogy.com/wpe24.jpg**.**Birth records**

The chart below shows the information contained in Irish birth records, as compared to those for England and Wales:

Information	Ireland	England & Wales
Date and place of birth	✓	✓
Forenames of child	✓	✓
Sex	✓	✓
Father's name	✓	✓
Father's address	✓	
Father's occupation	✓	✓
Mother's name	✓	✓
Mother's maiden surname	✓	✓
Mother's address	✓	
Name and address of person registering the birth	✓	✓

Death records

Irish death records contain the following information:

Information	Ireland	England & Wales
Date and place of death	✓	✓
Name	✓	✓
Sex	✓	✓
Marital status	✓	Note
Age at last birthday	✓	✓
Occupation	✓	✓
Cause of Death	✓	✓
Name and address of person registering the death	✓	✓

Note:

Although the death records of England and Wales do not specify the deceased's marital status, the name and occupation of a married woman's husband (even if he has predeceased her) are usually given in the space for 'occupation'.

Marriage records

An Irish marriage record gives the date and place of marriage, and for each party:

Information	Ireland	England & Wales
Age	✓	✓
Name	✓	✓
Marital status	✓	✓
Occupation	✓	✓
Address before marriage	✓	✓
Father's name and occupation	✓	✓

Ordering a certificate online from the Irish Republic

Republic of Ireland civil registration records are not available to view or download online. However, at the website of the Irish Republic's Health Service Executive (HSE) **www.hse.ie/eng/services/find_a_service/bdm/certificates_ie**, you can apply for a certificate for an event registered in the Irish Free State/Republic:

- Births from 1922;
- Marriages from 1922;
- Deaths from 1924.

You can also order a certificate from the HSE for an event registered in the whole of Ireland:

- Births from January 1864 to December 1921;
- Marriages from January 1920 to December 1921.

Certificates cost €10 each. This includes a search fee of €2, so if you want more than one copy of a specific certificate, the additional copies will cost €8 each. Postage costs €1 within the Irish Republic or the United Kingdom.

Ordering a certificate online from Northern Ireland

Birth, marriages and death records for Northern Ireland are to be digitised and the images made available online in 2013. This will be on a similar basis to the Scottish civil registration records available at the ScotlandsPeople website **www.scotlandspeople.gov.uk**, i.e. births up to 100 years ago, marriages to 75 years ago, and deaths to 50 years ago.

Meanwhile, at the NI Direct site **www.nidirect.gov.uk/gro**, you can order a certificate for an event that took place in what is now Northern Ireland:

- Births from 1864;
- Marriages from 1845 (for non-Catholic marriages) and 1864 (for all marriages) - for marriages before 1922, you need to supply the names of the church and district;
- Deaths from 1864.

The cost of a certificate is £14 (with postage free of charge in the United Kingdom), with additional copies costing a further £8 each.

Ordering a certificate by post

Alternatively, you can download an appropriate order form from either the GRO Ireland website **www.groireland.ie/apply_for_a_cert.htm** or from NI Direct **www.nidirect.gov.uk/gro** in 'Ordering certificates' (do it online section) and send your application by post.

The cost of ordering a certificate by post from the Republic of Ireland or Northern Ireland is the same as ordering one online. However, instead of a legally-admissible certificate, from the Irish Republic you can order a photocopy of the register entry for €6 (with extra copies costing €4).

Problems with online applications

Unfortunately, neither the Irish Republic's GRO nor GRONI is properly geared up to receive online applications from family historians. Both register offices require you to supply them with some of the information you're probably looking for, such as the address of the person and the name(s) of their parents or spouse.

When you apply online, neither register office allows you to specify the registration district, volume number and page number that you can obtain from the Irish birth, marriage or death index. The postal application forms are similar to the online application forms, but you can at least add a note about the index information, whereas the online systems will not allow you to apply if any information is missing.

Civil registration indexes

You can search the birth, marriage and death indexes for all of Ireland from 1845/1864 up to the end of 1921, as well as for the Irish Free State/Republic from 1922-1958 at the free LDS Church FamilySearch website **www.familysearch.org** and at the subscription site **www.ancestry.co.uk**.

Also at FamilySearch, you can find the databases 'Ireland Births and Baptisms', 'Ireland Marriages' and 'Ireland Deaths' (all taken from the International Genealogical Index or IGI), which include Irish civil registration births from 1864-1866, non-Catholic marriages from 1845-1849 and some deaths in 1864, 1865 and 1870.

The LDS Church has also microfilmed most of the Irish civil registration records and indexes, which you can order and view at any of its Family History Centres, of which there are 96 in Britain, three in Northern Ireland and three in the Irish Republic.

Transcriptions of civil registration records

The Roots Ireland website **www.rootsireland.ie** contains transcriptions of many (but not all) civil registration births, marriages and deaths and church baptisms, marriages and burials for most of the 32 counties of Ireland.

Roots Ireland operates a pay-per-view credit-based system, under which searching is free of charge, viewing a page of up to 10 search results costs one credit, and viewing a record transcription costs 25 credits. The cost of credits becomes less as you buy more, so that 35 credits cost €5.00 to buy, whereas 750 credits cost €60.00.

You can search a free database of transcriptions of County Waterford civil registration deaths from 1 January 1864 to 31 December 1901 at Waterford County Library's website **www.waterfordcountylibrary.ie/familyhistory/deathregisters**.

The Ulster Historical Foundation **www.ancestryireland.co.uk** has searchable databases of the birth, marriage and death records for Counties Antrim and Down. As well as transcriptions of civil registration records from 1864-1921, the databases also hold earlier records from church registers. Basic searching is free, but there is a charge of four credits to view transcriptions of the records, while members of the Foundation's Ulster Genealogical Historical Guild pay only two. The cost of credits varies from two for £2 up to 112 for £48.

The subscription website Emerald Ancestors **www.emeraldancestors.com** has a database that includes many church and civil records for the six counties of Northern Ireland. Civil births cover the years 1864-1876 and civil marriages 1845-1920. The 'death records' from 1803-1900 in the database are mainly an index of will calendars for the counties of Northern Ireland plus Donegal, Louth and Monaghan.

CHAPTER THREE
Census Returns

Although the first official census of Ireland was taken in 1821, only the 1901 and 1911 census returns still exist in their entirety. Unfortunately, the details of the 1861-1891 censuses were destroyed officially, and then the 1821-1851 census returns were lost in the fire at the Public Record Office of Ireland (PROI) in 1922.

At **http://homepage.eircom.net/~seanjmurphy/nai/censusmemo.htm**, you can read an interesting 'Memorandum on the Fate of the Destroyed Returns of the Census of Ireland 1861-91' written in 2001 by Sean Murphy of the Centre for Irish Genealogical and Historical Studies.

Some fragments and abstracts of the 1821-1871 censuses have survived, but of the 1881 and 1891 censuses there is unfortunately nothing at all remaining. There have been proposals to make the 1926 census of the Irish Free State (none was taken in 1921) available in the Republic of Ireland earlier than the official 100-year limit.

1821 census

In England, Wales and Scotland, the first official census was taken in 1801, but it wasn't until 1841 that people's names were included (apart from the relatively few places where the enumerators were - luckily for family historians - more diligent than they were required to be).

In Ireland, however, more information was supplied in 1821 than in Britain in 1841. All the inhabitants of 'townlands' (parish sub-divisions) were listed, with name, age, occupation and relationship to the head of the household. In addition, the number of storeys of the house, and the size of the family's land-holding in acres were given, but people's birthplaces were not.

1831 census

The census of Ireland carried out in 1831 provided much the same information as in 1821, but with the addition of a person's religious denomination (Established Church = Church of Ireland, Roman Catholic, Presbyterian or Other - Methodist, Baptist, etc.) and without the number of house storeys.

Both the National Archives of Ireland (NAI), which took over the functions of the PROI and the State Paper Office in 1988, and the Public Record Office of Northern Ireland (PRONI) in Belfast hold copies of a listing for County Derry/Londonderry, which had been thought to be part of the 1831 census.

It turns out, however, that this heads-of-household listing is part of a religious census of Ireland that was carried out in 1834 by the Commissioners of Public Instruction, based on the 1831 census.

Below is an example of what this '1831 census' contains (from the parish of Aghadowey in County Derry/Londonderry), taken from a microfilm copy held by the Society of Genealogists:

Townland	Head of household	No. of males	No. of females	Male servants	Female servants	Total	Estab lished	Rom. Cath. church	Pres byter ian	Other
Carn-rallagh	David Roxborough	6	6	-	-	12	-	-	12	-
Ditto	William Roxborough	1	1	-	-	2	-	-	2	
Ditto	William Roxborough Junior	3	5	-	-	8	-	-	8	-
Crevolea	James Roxborough	3	4	-	-	7	-	-	7	-
Ditto	David Roxborough	1	2	-	-	3	-	-	3	-

1841 and 1851 censuses

In 1841, the census of Ireland - recorded by householders and not enumerators - dropped the question on religious denomination, but did ask about the date of a person's marriage and whether people could read or write, as well as asking about members of the family who were absent or had died since the previous census. The question on religious denomination was restored in the 1851 census, which was otherwise the same as the previous census.

The only parish in Ireland for which the manuscript returns for 1841 have survived is Killeshandra in County Cavan. Many of the original 1851 manuscript returns for County Antrim have survived (and are at the NAI and the PRONI), as have various transcripts for other areas. The NAI and PRONI also have the results of official searches that were made in the 1841 and 1851 census records between 1908 and 1922 when old age pensions were introduced.

1861 and 1871 censuses

All that remains of these censuses are a transcript of the 1861 census for the parish of Enniscorthy in County Wexford (Roman Catholics only), and transcripts of the 1871 census for the parishes of Drumcondra and Loughbraclen in County Meath.

1881 and 1891 censuses

There are unfortunately no surviving manuscript returns of these censuses, and neither transcripts nor abstracts.

1901 and 1911 censuses

Returns for the whole of Ireland do exist in their entirety for the 1901 and 1911 censuses and these have been made public (as long ago as 1961 in the Irish Republic). The returns for both censuses give name, relationship to head of family, religion, ability to read or write, age, sex, marital status, birthplace, whether able to speak Irish, and if deaf, dumb, blind, 'imbecile', 'idiot' or 'lunatic'. Although birthplace was included in the census questionnaire, only the county or city of birth was required.

As in Britain, the Irish 1911 census also provides information on how long a current marriage had lasted, how many children had been born alive within that marriage and how many of those children were still alive.

Irish census records online

Images of the Irish 1901 and 1911 census records have been digitised and indexed and are available free of charge at **www.census.nationalarchives.ie.** The site also has illustrated articles describing the cities of Dublin and Belfast and Counties Cork, Galway, Kerry and Waterford.

Prior to the national release of the censuses, some local indexed transcriptions had been produced and are still available. You'll find the 1901 census for all of Counties Leitrim, Mayo, Roscommon and Sligo, and about 25% of County Wexford at the free Leitrim-Roscommon Genealogy Website **www.leitrim-roscommon.com,** while the 1901 census of County Clare is at the free Clare County Library site **www.clarelibrary.ie/eolas/coclare/genealogy/genealog.htm**.

Irish Origins **www.irishorigins.com**, a subscription-based website, includes databases of the 1901 census of the Rotunda ward in Dublin; 60,000 Dublin heads of household, extracted from the 1851 census; and a census carried out in 1749 in the Diocese of Elphin (51 of the 59 parishes of County Roscommon, plus 13 parishes in County Sligo and eight in County Galway).

The subscription-based site Ancestry.co.uk **www.ancestry.co.uk** has many Irish databases, including an indexed transcription of the 1851 census of part of County Antrim (enumerating about 28,000 people) and four parishes in County Cork. In addition, the site has databases containing information abstracted from the 1841 and 1851 censuses in connection with applications for old age pensions.

At the website **www.ireland-genealogy.com** (formerly **www.pensear.org**), you can carry out a free search of the pension information from the 1841 and 1851 censuses held by the PRONI for the six counties that are now Northern Ireland, as well as for County Donegal. You can then order a copy of the record on a payment basis.

At the free Census Finder website **www.censusfinder.com/ireland.htm**, you'll find links to sites with transcripts of fragments of the 1821 census for parts of Counties Cavan, Cork, Fermanagh, Leitrim, Tipperary and Waterford; the '1831 census' of the parish of Dunboe, County Derry/Londonderry; parts of the 1851 census of Counties Antrim, Cork and Waterford; and some other unofficial censuses and other population lists.

The Ulster Ancestry website **www.ulsterancestry.com/ua-free-pages.php** includes 'free pages' with abstracts from the 1821, 1841 and 1851 censuses of the parish of

Killymard, County Donegal, as well as transcriptions of the 1851 census for part of County Antrim.

The pay-per-view site Roots Ireland **www.rootsireland.ie** has transcripts of the 1821 census for parts of Counties Armagh, Cavan, Galway, Kilkenny and Offaly; the 1831 census for part of County Kilkenny; the 1841 census of parts of Counties Cavan and Galway; and unofficial censuses taken in a parish of County Westmeath in 1835 and parishes in County Galway in 1834, 1884 and 1895.

You can find an index of names listed in the 1831/1834 heads-of-household census of County Derry/Londonderry at Bill Macafee's Family and Local History Website **www.billmacafee.com**. The site includes a number of other databases covering that county, as well as the north and central parts of County Antrim.

The library of the Society of Genealogists

In the Society's library, you'll find a microfilmed copy of the '1831 census' for most of County Derry/Londonderry, as well as an index on CD. For County Cavan, the library holds copies on microfilm of the 1821 census of parts of Munterconnaught, Lurgan and Mullagh; the 1841 census of part of Killeshandra; and a CD with parts of the 1831 and 1841 censuses.

In addition, the SoG has copies (in *The Irish Ancestor*) of the 1821 census of Aglish & Portnascully and Iverk, and the 1841 and 1851 censuses of Aglish (all in County Kilkenny). Also in *The Irish Ancestor*, the society has a census of Protestants in Shanrahan & Tullagherton in County Tipperary in 1864-1870.

The library also holds (in *The Irish Genealogist*) extracts of the 1821 census for the City of Waterford, and an 1867 census of Marshallstown in County Wexford.

CENSUS OF IRELAND, 1901.

(Two Examples of the mode of filling up this Table are given on the other side.)

FORM A.

No. on Form B. /

RETURN of the MEMBERS of this FAMILY and their VISITORS, BOARDERS, SERVANTS, &c., who slept or abode in this House on the night of SUNDAY, the 31st of MARCH, 1901.

No.	NAME and SURNAME (Christian Name)	Surname	RELATION to Head of Family	RELIGIOUS PROFESSION	EDUCATION	AGE (Years on last Birth-day)		SEX	RANK, PROFESSION, OR OCCUPATION	MARRIAGE	WHERE BORN	IRISH LANGUAGE	If Deaf and Dumb; Dumb only; Blind; Imbecile or Idiot; or Lunatic
						Males	Females						
1	Kate	McMahon	Head of Family	Roman Catholic	Read, Write	63		F	Farmer	Widow	Co. Clare	Irish & English	
2	Joseph	McMahon	Son	Roman Catholic	Read, Write	36		M	Farmer's Son	Not married	Co. Clare	Irish & English	
3	Mary	McMahon	Daughter	Roman Catholic	Read, Write	31		F	Spinster	Not married	Co. Clare	Irish	
4	Barnard	McMahon	Son	Roman Catholic	Read, Write	32		M	Farmer's Son	Not married	Co. Clare	Irish & English	
5													
6													
7													
8													
9													
10													
11													
12													
13													
14													
15													

I hereby certify, as required by the Act 63 Vic., cap. 6, s. 6 (1), that the foregoing Return is correct, according to the best of my knowledge and belief

Isaac Mill Coogh (Signature of Enumerator.)

.I believe the foregoing to be a true Return.

Kate McMahon (Signature of Head of Family).

I. National Archives of Ireland (NAI), Census 1901, DED Kiltoraght, Co. Clare, Form A return for the household of Kate McMahon.

CENSUS OF IRELAND, 1911.

Two Examples of the mode of filling up this Table are given on the other side.

FORM A.

No. on Form B. 30

RETURN of the MEMBERS of this FAMILY and their VISITORS, BOARDERS, SERVANTS, &c., who slept or abode in this House on the night of SUNDAY, the 2nd of APRIL, 1911.

No.	NAME AND SURNAME (Christian Name)	Surname	RELATION to Head of Family	RELIGIOUS PROFESSION	EDUCATION	Ages of Males	Ages of Females	RANK, PROFESSION, OR OCCUPATION	Whether "Married," "Widower," "Widow," or "Single"	Completed years the present Marriage has lasted	Total Children born alive	Children still living	WHERE BORN	IRISH LANGUAGE	If Deaf and Dumb, Blind, Imbecile or Idiot, or Lunatic
1	John	Turtle	Head	Meth.? Church	Read and write	44		Labourer in the Foundry General	Married				Belfast		—
2	Grace	Turtle	Wife	Episcopalian	Read and write		37		Married	4	2	2	Belfast		—
3	Victor	Turtle	Son	Church of Ireland	Cannot Read	4		—	Single				Belfast		—
4	Adelaide	Turtle	Daughter	Church of Ireland	Read and Write		1	—	Single				Belfast		—
5	Isabella	Law	Servant	Church of Ireland	Read and Write			Laundress	Single				Belfast		—
6	Sarah	Law	Servant	Church of Ireland	Read and Write		33	Yarn Reeler	Single				Belfast		—
7															
8															
9															
10															
11															
12															
13															
14															
15															

I hereby certify, as required by the Act 10 Edw. VII., and 1 Geo. V., cap. 11, that the foregoing Return is correct, according to the best of my knowledge and belief.

_____ Signature of Enumerator.

I believe the foregoing to be a true Return.

John Turtle Signature of Head of Family.

2. National Archives of Ireland (NAI), Census 1911, DED Wood Vale Ward (Belfast), Co. Antrim, Form A return for the household of John Turtle.

Sir Richard Griffith before 1875.

CHAPTER FOUR
Census Substitutes

Because so little remains of the Irish 19th-century censuses, other population listings take their place to a certain extent. Although there are no other records that list the entire population of Ireland, there are some heads-of-household listings. The most useful of these - because it lists around 1.3 million heads of households, whether in towns or in the country - is Griffith's Valuation.

This is a land valuation that was carried out between 1847 and 1864 under the direction of Sir Richard Griffith (1784-1878), Director of the Valuation Office in Dublin. The Tithe Applotment Books were a similar valuation, carried out between 1823 and 1838, but listing about a million heads of household, as the survey excluded towns. The records of the Landed Estates Court from 1850-1885 contain information on about 8,000 bankrupt estates with over half a million tenants.

There are also many other population lists, some covering quite small geographical areas.

Griffith's Valuation (1847-1864)

The Primary Valuation of Tenements, to give the survey its official name, was carried out to enable liability for the Poor Rate (to support the poor and

destitute of each area) to be calculated. The valuation was published in different years for different counties, beginning with County Dublin from 1847-1851 and ending with County Armagh in 1864.

The valuation lists all tenants and their landlords, and covers all of Ireland, both town and country. Because Griffith's Valuation is a heads-of-household listing, there are few women and no children in the list.

For each property, the valuation of each parish includes:

| Reference number on associated map |
| Townland (with street names in towns) |
| Occupier |
| Person from whom property leased |
| Description of property (such as 'house, office and garden', 'land' or 'bog') |
| Area (in acres, roods and perches) |
| Rateable annual valuation of land |
| Rateable annual valuation of buildings |
| Total annual valuation of rateable property |

Tithe Applotment Books (1823-1838)

The (Protestant) Church of Ireland was the established church in Ireland until 1870. As tithes payable to the Church of Ireland became payable in money rather than in kind from 1823 onwards, a valuation of Ireland was carried out from that time until 1838. The Tithe Applotment Books that resulted contain the names of occupiers of land on which tithes were payable, but don't list labourers or town-dwellers.

The Tithe Applotment Books are organised by parish, with information including:

| Occupier |
| Townland |
| Area in acres |
| Land classification |
| Amount of tithe due |

Landed estates records (1850-1885)

These records contain information on the tenants of the many Irish estates whose owners were declared bankrupt during the mid- to late-19th century. The lot descriptions contained in the records contain information on their ownership and occupation history, the size of the piece of land and the annual rent chargeable. They also include a list of tenants, with the size of their holdings and terms of tenure.

In cases where the tenant held land by lease, rather than by annual tenancy, the names will be given of all 'lives' (of which there were usually three) included in the contract, stating whether any of the lives were still living at the time of the sale. Lives were the people to whom a lease would pass in the event of the leaseholder's death, each of whom would retain it for the rest of his life.

The records of a landed estate usually included an estate map or town plan, often with a detailed map of the lot.

Freeholders' records (pre-1840)

The Public Record Office of Northern Ireland (PRONI) has published a database of records of freeholders in Ulster (mainly in the counties of Northern Ireland).

Freeholders were men who either owned or leased land, which entitled them to vote, although from 1727-1793 only Protestants with a freehold of 40 shillings (£2) a year were allowed to vote. From 1793, Roman Catholics with a forty-shilling freehold were also enfranchised, but in 1829, this was increased to £10 (for both Protestants and Catholics).

The PRONI database includes names taken from electoral rolls (which listed those men entitled to vote) and poll books (showing those men who had actually voted). The database records contain some of the following information:

Name of freeholder
Address of freeholder
Location of freehold
Description of freehold
Name of landlord
Address of landlord
Value of freehold
Names of other 'lives'
Date and place of freeholder's registration
Occupation of freeholder
Religion of freeholder
For whom the freeholder voted

Irish census substitutes online

You can search Griffith's Valuation free of charge at the Ask About Ireland website **www.askaboutireland.ie/griffith-valuation/index.xml**, which lets you view and print digitised pages from the original valuation schedules. You can also view online maps showing the boundaries of townlands in red and letting you see the location of the plots of land that your ancestors owned or rented. In addition, you can search by barony (similar to a hundred or wapentake in England), Poor Law Union or civil parish to get a list of all the heads of household who lived in each townland.

You can also view indexed digitised records of Griffith's Valuation (including maps and town plans) at the Irish Origins subscription website **www.irishorigins.com**, which also contains the William Smith O'Brien petition, signed by over 80,000 people (both in Ireland and in Britain) between October 1848 and May 1849. The petitioners successfully asked for clemency for O'Brien, a member of parliament who had been sentenced to death for leading an abortive uprising against the British Government. Irish Origins also has a database of Irish electoral registers covering the period 1832-1838.

The subscription site Ancestry.co.uk **www.ancestry.co.uk** has a database of Griffith's Valuation and an index of the Tithe Applotment Books. The Griffith's database includes digitised images of the valuation schedules, as well as black-and-white valuation maps. Beware, however, when using Ancestry's Tithe Applotment Book database, as this became very deficient in Northern Ireland records after it was updated to include records for what is now the Irish Republic. The problem has been reported to Ancestry.

At Ulster Ancestry **www.ulsterancestry.com/search.html**, you can carry out a free search in Griffith's Valuation for the nine counties of Ulster: Antrim, Armagh, Derry/Londonderry, Down, Fermanagh and Tyrone (all in Northern Ireland) and Cavan, Donegal and Monaghan (in the Irish Republic).

You'll find a database of information from Griffith's Valuation for parts of Galway, Leitrim, Mayo, Roscommon and Limerick at the free Leitrim-Roscommon Genealogy Website **www.leitrim-roscommon.com**.

At Clare County Library's free website **www.clarelibrary.ie/eolas/coclare/ genealogy/genealog.htm**, you can find many databases for the county, including indexes to Griffith's Valuation and transcriptions of the local Tithe Applotment Books.

In addition, Waterford County Library has a free online transcription of Griffith's Valuation for the county at **www.waterfordcountylibrary.ie/en/familyhistory/ griffithsvaluation**.

The Findmypast Ireland subscription/pay-per-view site **www.findmypast.ie** holds the Landed Estates Court Rentals, as well as Griffith's Valuation.

The free PRONI website **www.proni.gov.uk** has a database of freeholders, as well as a database of signatories to the Ulster Covenant and Ulster Declaration on 28 September 1912. The c.240,000 men who signed the covenant and a similar number of women who signed the declaration were opposed to Home Rule for Ireland.

You'll find many population databases, mainly for Counties Antrim and Down, at the subscription-based Ulster Historical Foundation site **www.ancestryireland.co.uk**.

The free Census Finder site **www.censusfinder.com/ireland.htm** has links to websites with a large variety of population listings, including Griffith's Valuation, the Tithe Applotment Books, muster rolls, electoral registers, hearth money rolls and lists of tenants, landowners, flax growers, tithe defaulters, teachers and pupils.

PARISH OF ANTRIM.

No. and Letters of Reference to Map.	Townlands and Occupiers.	Immediate Lessors.	Description of Tenement.	Area.	Rateable Annual Valuation. Land.	Rateable Annual Valuation. Buildings.	Total Annual Valuation of Rateable Property.
				A. R. P.	£ s. d.	£ s. d.	£ s. d.
	KILBEGS— *continued.*						
19	Belfast and Northern Counties Railway Company (*Charles Stewart, Secretary*),	In fee,	Railway (90 *lin. perches*),	2 0 24	—	—	47 5 0
20	John Frew,	Rev. William C. O'Neill,	Land,	11 1 4	8 10 0	—	8 10 0
			Total of Rateable Property,	504 0 9	515 5 0	103 0 0	665 10 0
			EXEMPTIONS :				
10		Rev. William C. O'Neill,	Grave-yard,	0 2 20	0 10 0	—	0 10 0
			Total, including Exemptions,	504 2 29	515 15 0	103 0 0	666 0 0
	CREEVERY. (*Ord. S. 44.*)						
1 a	Thomas Owens,	William Taggart,	House, offices, and land,	13 3 5	9 0 0	13 0 0	22 0 0
— b	David M'Collum,	Same,	House,	—	—	0 10 0	0 10 0
— c	Robert Kirk,	Same,	House,	—	—	0 10 0	0 10 0
— d	John M'Ilwrath,	Same,	House,	—	—	0 15 0	0 15 0
— e	Frances O'Hara,	Same,	House and shed,	—	—	0 15 0	0 15 0
— f	John Whiteside,	Same,	House and shed,	—	—	0 15 0	0 15 0
2	William Taggart,	Rev. William C. O'Neill,	House, offices, and land,	30 3 20	27 0 0	1 15 0	28 15 0
3 a	Joseph Taggart,	Same,	House, offices, and land,	25 2 20	20 10 0	2 15 0	23 5 0
— b	John Whiteside,	Joseph Taggart,	House,	—	—	0 10 0	0 10 0
4	Joseph Taggart,	Rev. William C. O'Neill,	Offices and land,	11 2 38	8 10 0	1 0 0	9 10 0
5	Thomas Craig,	Thomas Stewart,	House, offices, and land,	9 2 5	6 0 0	0 15 0	6 15 0
6	Esther Agnew,	Rev. William C. O'Neill,	House, offices, and land,	8 1 15	5 0 0	0 10 0	5 10 0
7 A a }	James Buck,	Same,	House, offices, & land, {	14 1 25	8 10 0	0 15 0	} 10 10 0
— B				1 0 30	1 5 0	—	
7 b	National School-house and play-ground,	(*See Exemptions.*)					
8	Anthony Wilson,	Rev. William C. O'Neill,	House, offices, and land,	32 2 20	23 0 0	1 10 0	24 10 0
9 a	John Orr,	Same,	Herd's house and land,	17 3 5	9 10 0	0 10 0	10 0 0
— b	Peter Moreton,	John Orr,	House,	—	—	0 10 0	0 10 0
10	Samuel Orr,	Rev. William C. O'Neill,	House, offices, and land,	16 2 20	11 5 0	1 5 0	12 10 0
11	John Denison,	Same,	House, offices, and land,	38 3 35	30 10 0	1 10 0	32 0 0
12	James Scott,	Same,	House, offices, and land,	13 2 25	10 10 0	1 10 0	12 0 0
13 a	Samuel Kirk,	Same,	House, offices, and land,	37 0 35	28 15 0	5 0 0	33 15 0
— b	William Fletcher,	Samuel Kirk,	House, office, & garden,	0 1 15	0 10 0	0 15 0	1 5 0
14	Samuel Kirk,	Rev. William C. O'Neill,	Land,	32 0 20	12 5 0	—	12 5 0
15	Patrick Fox,	Same,	House, offices, and land,	44 3 5	29 15 0	1 5 0	31 0 0
16 a	John M'Cracken,	Same,	House, offices, and land,	43 1 15	28 15 0	2 0 0	30 15 0
— b	John Vance,	John M'Cracken,	House,	—	—	0 15 0	0 15 0
— c	Daniel Taggart,	Same,	House,	—	—	0 5 0	0 5 0
17	William Davison,	Rev. William C. O'Neill,	Herd's ho., off., & land,	40 3 20	18 10 0	0 15 0	19 5 0
18	William Taylor,	Same,	House, offices, and land,	33 1 25	14 10 0	1 10 0	16 0 0
19	John M'Keown,	Same,	Land,	4 3 25	2 5 0	—	2 5 0
20	Alexander Campbell,	Same,	House, offices, and land,	16 3 30	8 0 0	1 5 0	9 5 0
21	Hugh Moore,	Same,	Herd's ho., off., & land,	26 2 10	15 0 0	0 15 0	15 15 0
			Total of Rateable Property,	515 2 23	328 15 0	45 5 0	374 0 0
			EXEMPTIONS :				
7 b		Rev. William C. O'Neill,	National School-house and play-ground,	0 0 30	0 5 0	1 15 0	2 0 0
			Total, including Exemptions,	515 3 13	329 0 0	47 0 0	376 0 0
	KILGAVANAGH. (*Ord. S. 44.*)						
1	John M'Keown,	Rev. William C. O'Neill,	House, offices, and land,	63 1 10	20 15 0	2 0 0	22 15 0
2	William Miller,	Same,	House, offices, and land,	38 3 34	24 0 0	1 10 0	25 10 0
3	Daniel Carlisle,	Same,	House, offices, and land,	28 0 25	24 5 0	1 10 0	25 15 0
4	Joseph M'Lenahan,	Same,	House, offices, and land,	27 1 15	23 5 0	1 0 0	24 5 0
5 A a }	James Agnew,	Same,	House, offices, & land, {	15 0 24	12 10 0	1 0 0	} 14 15 0
— B				1 0 30	1 5 0	—	

3. Griffith's Valuation schedule 1862, County Antrim, Parish of Antrim.

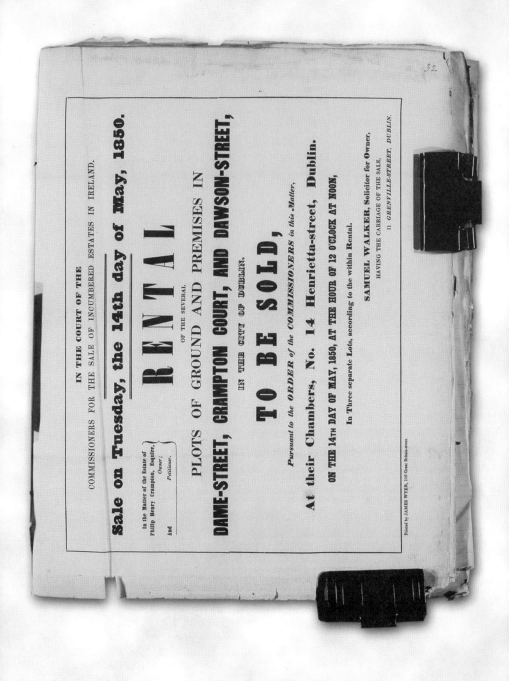

IN THE COURT OF THE

COMMISSIONERS FOR THE SALE OF INCUMBERED ESTATES IN IRELAND.

Sale on Tuesday, the 14th day of May, 1850.

RENTAL

OF THE SEVERAL

PLOTS OF GROUND AND PREMISES IN

DAME-STREET, CRAMPTON COURT, AND DAWSON-STREET,

IN THE CITY OF DUBLIN,

TO BE SOLD,

Pursuant to the ORDER of the COMMISSIONERS in this Matter,

At their Chambers, No. 14 Henrietta-street, Dublin,

ON THE 14TH DAY OF MAY, 1850, AT THE HOUR OF 12 O'CLOCK AT NOON,

In Three separate Lots, according to the within Rental.

In the Matter of the Estate of Philip Henry Crampton, Esquire, Owner; And Petitioner.

SAMUEL WALKER, Solicitor for Owner, HAVING THE CARRIAGE OF THE SALE, 11 GRENVILLE-STREET, DUBLIN.

Printed by JAMES WYER, 116 Great Britain-street.

4. Advertisement for the sale of a Landed Estate in Dame Street, Crampton Court and Dawson Street in the City of Dublin in 1850.

THE CRAMPTON COURT PROPERTY.—*Continued.*

Denomination.	Tenants' Names.	Tenants' Yearly Rents.	Gale Days.	Head Rent.	Particulars of Tenant and Tenants' Leases.	OBSERVATIONS.
		£ s. d.				
		Forward's 332 5 5				
Dwelling-house, No. 20 Crampton Court.	Jane Glynn, widow, representative of Patrick Farrell.	6 6 0	25th March, 29th September.		Lease dated 14th August, 1819, to Patrick Farrell, for three lives (all now in being), viz., the lessee, Patrick Farrell, Joanna Farrell, then aged 16 years, and William Farrell, then aged 4 years.	There is a covenant in this lease, that in case any of the said lives shall at any time leave or depart from Ireland, and that the Lessee shall not produce such person to the Lessor, the life of such person or persons shall be considered extinct, with liberty to the Lessee to nominate another life, or other lives instead, provided such life or lives shall not be younger than the person or persons in whose place he or they shall be substituted.
Dwelling-house, No. 18 Crampton Court.	Mark J. Pattison.	20 0 0	1st February, 1st May, 1st August, 1st Nov.		Lease dated 6th May, 1890, to said Mark J. Pattison, for three lives (all now in being), viz., the Queen, Charles William Marquis of Kildare, and Charles James Duke of Leinster, or for a term of 31 years from 1st May, 1829.	There is a small yard at rere of this house. This lease reserves a larger rent; but by an indorsement thereon, dated 10th February, 1849, the rent was reduced to £20, and a clause of surrender given at the end of every three years; also a clause against alienation.
Dwelling-house, No. 19 Crampton Court.	Bartholomew Rorke.	12 0 0	1st May, 1st November.		Yearly tenant from 1st May, 1846, by memorandum in writing, dated 10th June, 1846.	The rent reserved was £15, but it was afterwards (verbally) abated to £12.
Dwelling-house, No. 17 Crampton Court.	Alexander S. Stewart.	28 0 0	10th February, 10th August.		Yearly tenant from 10th February, 1850, by verbal agreement.	There is a small yard at rere of this house. This rent is inclusive of all taxes, which are about £8 10s. per annum.
Billiard Rooms, Crampton Court.	Unlet.	5 0 0				The entry to these rooms is through No. 17. The passage through No. 76 Dame-street leads to these rooms, through which passage there is a right of entry. This rent is a valuation rent.
Dwelling-house, No. 16 Crampton Court.	Isaac Dwyer.	14 0 0	1st February, 1st May, 1st August, 1st Nov.		Quarterly tenant from 1st November, 1849, by verbal agreement.	This rent is inclusive of all taxes, which are about £4 10s. Since the final Notice was served on this tenant he has sent the keys of the house to the landlord.
Dwelling-house, No. 15 Crampton Court.	Joseph Menhang.	6 6 0	1st of each month.		Monthly tenant, commencing 1st February, 1850, by verbal agreement.	This rent is inclusive of all taxes, which are about £9 per annum. This house is in bad repair.
Dwelling-houses, No. 14 Crampton Court.	Christopher Fitzgerald.	18 0 0	10th of each month.		Monthly tenant by memorandum in writing, dated 12th August, 1849.	This rent is inclusive of all taxes, which are about £9 per annum. A higher rent was reserved, but afterwards reduced.
Dwelling-house, No. 13 Crampton Court.	Unlet.	8 0 0	1st January, 1st April, 1st July, 1st October.			This house is out of repair. The rent mentioned is a valuation rent.
Dwelling-house, No. 12 Crampton Court.	Henry Connell.	36 0 0	1st January, 1st April, 1st July, 1st October.		Lease dated 25th February, 1847, to said Henry Connell, for a term of 21 years from 1st January, 1847.	

Head Rent column note: To be indemnified against by Purchasers of Dame-street Property.

	£ s. d.
Gross Rental, ...	£ 285 11 6
Deduct amount of Taxes included in Rents payable for Houses Nos. 13, 14, 15, 16, 17, and premises in Stable-yard, about ...	40 11 6
Nett Rental, ...	£ 245 0 0

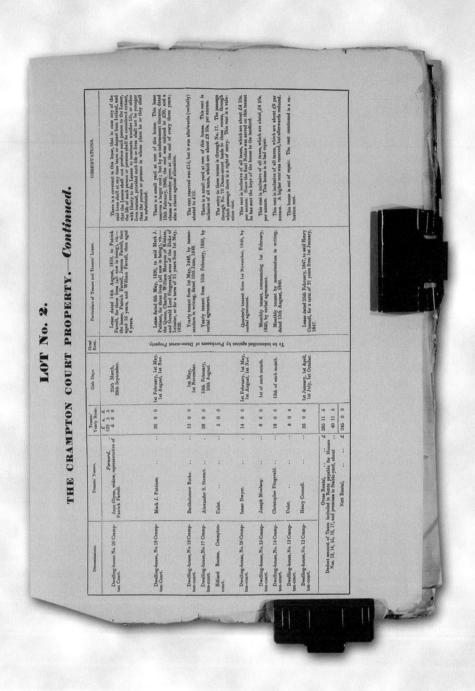

5. Landed Estate Court Rental 1850, Crampton Court, City of Dublin.

CHAPTER FIVE
Church Registers

The established church in Ireland until 1870 was the Church of Ireland, a Protestant church in the Anglican Communion. The church instructed its clergy to record baptisms, marriages and burials in parish registers as early as 1634, and two registers were begun even earlier.

There are surviving registers for only four Church of Ireland parishes dating from before 1650: St. John, Dublin (from 1619); Blaris, Lisburn, County Antrim (from 1637); Templemore, County Derry/Londonderry (from 1642); and Holy Trinity, Cork (from 1643). The registers of 45 parishes begin between 1650 and 1700, just over 200 begin in the 18th century, and about 340 in the early 19th century.

The majority of Irishmen and women worshipped not in the Church of Ireland, but in the Roman Catholic Church, whose earliest surviving register is that of Wexford, beginning in 1671. Many Catholic registers don't start until the mid-19th century, however. This is particularly so in the rural north and west of Ireland.

In the 16th and 17th centuries, the province of Ulster was 'planted' with Scottish and English settlers, the ancestors of the Protestants living in Northern Ireland today. Most of the Scots were Presbyterians, whose Irish churches began keeping registers about 1700.

The fire in the Public Record Office of Ireland (PROI) in 1922 caused the destruction of about 60% of the PROI's holding of Church of Ireland parish registers - which had been called in for safe keeping!

Of the registers at the PROI, only those of the parishes of:

- Ballyclough, County Cork, from 1831-1900;
- Castletownroche, County Cork, from 1728-1804, and vestry minutes from 1724-1809;
- Clogherny, County Tyrone, baptisms from 1859-1875;
- Nobber, County Meath, from 1828-1869;

survived the destruction.

Luckily, many of the registers had been copied, so that around 50% of Church of Ireland registers are still in existence, either as originals or transcriptions.

The Irish equivalents of bishops' transcripts are known as parochial returns, which were instituted (together with parish registers) in 1634. Unfortunately, the parochial returns were also held at the PROI, and almost all were destroyed in the 1922 fire. The only surviving returns were those for the parishes of:

- Innismacsaint, County Fermanagh, from 1660-1866;
- Inniskeel, County Donegal, from 1699-1700 and 1818-1864;
- St. Mary, Dublin, from 1831-1870.

In the Irish Republic, both the National Archives of Ireland (the successor to the PROI) and the Representative Church Body Library (the official repository of Church of Ireland registers in the Irish Republic) - both in Dublin - hold copies of nearly all the surviving pre-1870 Church of Ireland registers. The National Library of Ireland, also in Dublin, has copies of almost all Roman Catholic registers up to 1880.

Copies of Church of Ireland, Presbyterian, Roman Catholic and other registers for Northern Ireland are held by the Public Record Office of Northern Ireland (PRONI) in Belfast. You'll find a downloadable *Guide to Church Records* at **www.proni.gov.uk/guide_to_church_records.pdf**

Most church registers have been transcribed and indexed by Ireland's county-based family history research centres, most of which are members of the Irish Family History Foundation (IFHF). The records are now available online at the Roots Ireland website **www.rootsireland.ie** (see below).

In the early 19th century, especially from 1820, pro-forma baptism and burial registers began to be used that were similar to those introduced in England and Wales in 1813. Prior to their introduction, baptism records tended to state only the names of the child and parents and the date of baptism. The new pro-forma baptism registers had, in addition, columns for the date of birth, 'abode', and 'quality, trade or profession'.

Pro-forma marriage registers were also introduced, in which were entered - in addition to the names of the bride and groom and the date of marriage - the addresses of both parties (although this was often just the name of the parish) and the names and addresses of witnesses.

Early burial records tend to state only the name of the deceased and date of death, whereas the pro-forma burial registers give name, abode, when buried, and age.

Printed copies of registers

The Representative Church Body Library has published early Church of Ireland registers for the churches of:

Cathedral Church of St. Columb, Derry, 1703-32 and 1732-75
Cathedral of St. Fin Barre, Cork, 1753-1804
Cathedral of St. Patrick, Dublin, 1677-1869
Holy Trinity, Cork, 1643-1668
Leixlip Parish, County Kildare, 1665-1778
St. Catherine, Dublin, 1636-1715
St. John the Evangelist, Dublin, 1619-1699
St. Nicholas, Galway, 1792-1840
St. Thomas, Dublin, 1750-1791
St. Thomas, Lisnagarvey, County Antrim, 1637-1646
Shankill Parish, Belfast, 1745-1761

Church registers online

The FamilySearch website **www.familysearch.org** holds databases of more than five million Irish births and baptisms from 1620-1881, over 400,000 marriages from 1619-1898 and over 50,000 deaths from 1864-1870. You can find out which Irish parishes are covered at Canadian genealogist Hugh Wallis's website **http://freepages.genealogy.rootsweb.ancestry.com/~hughwallis** or at Steve Archer's similar site **www.archersoftware.co.uk/igi/index.htm** (only a few counties so far).

The IFHF's Roots Ireland pay-per-view website **www.rootsireland.ie** has indexed transcriptions of Roman Catholic and Church of Ireland baptisms, marriages and burials for most Irish counties. There are also (for some counties) Baptist, Congregational, Methodist, Quaker (Religious Society of Friends) and Presbyterian records.

Most of the counties that are not included in the Roots Ireland databases are to be found on the Irish Government's free Irish Genealogy website **www.irishgenealogy.ie**. There you'll find indexed transcriptions and, in many cases, digital images of the records too.

The Ulster Historical Foundation's Ancestry Ireland subscription website **www.ancestryireland.com** includes many Roman Catholic, Church of Ireland and Presbyterian baptism, marriage and burial records from the church registers of Counties Antrim and Down (also on Roots Ireland). Access to these records is provided on a pay-per-view basis, with a discount for subscribers.

The subscription website Emerald Ancestors **www.emeraldancestors.com** has a database that includes many church and civil records for the six counties of Northern Ireland. Church baptisms cover the period 1796-1924 and church marriages 1823-1901. The 'death records' from 1803-1900 in the database are mainly an index of will calendars for the counties of Northern Ireland plus Donegal, Louth and Monaghan.

County Clare is the only county whose church registers are included in neither the Roots Ireland nor the Irish Genealogy databases. However, you can view transcriptions of 19th century marriages (from 1837) and baptisms (from 1841) in the parish of Ennis at the free Ennis Parish website **www.ennisparish.com/genealogy**. The transcriptions have been carried out by the Clare Roots Society, as have some other church record transcriptions, which you can find at the free Clare County Library site **www.clarelibrary.ie/eolas/coclare/genealogy/genealog.htm**.

Although two of Cork City's Roman Catholic churches are included with south Cork in the Irish Genealogy database, the Cork Ancestral Project has digitised many other Roman Catholic registers, but has not yet made any information available online. Cork County Library has a copy of the project's index of baptism and marriage records for the parish of St Mary and St Anne.

Cork City's Church of Ireland registers are being computerised by the Cobh Genealogical Project **www.cork.anglican.org/resources/genealogy.html**, but these too are not yet available online. You can request (by letter) a search in the database and microfilmed registers, however.

The following table shows which counties are included in the various databases:

County	Database	Website
Antrim	Roots Ireland Ulster Historical Foundation Emerald Ancestors	www.rootsireland.ie www.ancestryireland.com www.emeraldancestors.com
Armagh	Roots Ireland Emerald Ancestors	www.rootsireland.ie www.emeraldancestors.com
Carlow	Irish Genealogy	www.irishgenealogy.ie
Cavan	Roots Ireland	www.rootsireland.ie
Clare	Ennis Parish Clare County Library	www.ennisparish.com/genealogy www.clarelibrary.ie
Cork City	Some at Irish Genealogy	www.irishgenealogy.ie
Cork, north	Roots Ireland	www.rootsireland.ie
Cork, south	Irish Genealogy	www.irishgenealogy.ie
Derry/Londonderry	Roots Ireland Emerald Ancestors	www.rootsireland.ie www.emeraldancestors.com
Donegal	Roots Ireland	www.rootsireland.ie
Down	Roots Ireland Ulster Historical Foundation Emerald Ancestors	www.rootsireland.ie www.ancestryireland.com www.emeraldancestors.com
Dublin City	Irish Genealogy	www.irishgenealogy.ie
Dublin (rest of county)	Roots Ireland	www.rootsireland.ie
Fermanagh	Roots Ireland Emerald Ancestors	www.rootsireland.ie www.emeraldancestors.com
Galway	Roots Ireland	www.rootsireland.ie
Kerry	Irish Genealogy	www.irishgenealogy.ie
Kildare	Roots Ireland	www.rootsireland.ie
Kilkenny	Roots Ireland	www.rootsireland.ie
Laois	Roots Ireland	www.rootsireland.ie
Leitrim	Roots Ireland	www.rootsireland.ie
Limerick	Roots Ireland	www.rootsireland.ie
Longford	Roots Ireland	www.rootsireland.ie
Louth	Roots Ireland	www.rootsireland.ie
Mayo	Roots Ireland	www.rootsireland.ie
Meath	Roots Ireland	www.rootsireland.ie
Monaghan	Roots Ireland	www.rootsireland.ie
Offaly	Roots Ireland	www.rootsireland.ie
Roscommon	Roots Ireland	www.rootsireland.ie
Sligo	Roots Ireland	www.rootsireland.ie
Tipperary	Roots Ireland	www.rootsireland.ie
Tyrone	Roots Ireland Emerald Ancestors	www.rootsireland.ie www.emeraldancestors.com

County	Database	Website
Waterford	Roots Ireland	www.rootsireland.ie
Westmeath	Roots Ireland	www.rootsireland.ie
Wexford	Roots Ireland	www.rootsireland.ie
Wicklow	Roots Ireland	www.rootsireland.ie

At the Ancestry.co.uk site **www.ancestry.co.uk**, you'll find indexes to many Roman Catholic baptisms from 1742-1881, marriages and banns from 1742-1884 and burials from 1756-1881.

The website Findmypast Ireland **www.findmypast.ie** includes the registers of Derry Cathedral from 1642-1703, some French non-conformist churches in Dublin from 1701-1831, St Patrick's Cathedral in Dublin from 1677-1800, and the French church at Portarlington in County Laois from 1694-1816.

The CMC (christening, marriage, and cemetery) Record Project site **www.cmcrp.net** contains searchable volunteer transcriptions of birth, marriage, death, cemetery, land and property records. These principally cover Counties Clare, Cork, Dublin, Kerry, Limerick, Mayo, Tipperary, Waterford, Wexford and Wicklow (but also include an 1821 census remnant for County Cavan).

IGP (Ireland Genealogy Projects) is a group of county-based websites with transcriptions of family history records. You can find the transcripts, which include church, cemetery and gravestone records, in the IGP Archives **www.igp-web.com/IGPArchives/index.htm**

BAPTISMS

SOLEMNIZED IN THE MILITARY CHURCH, ARBOUR HILL, IN THE YEAR 1849

No.	When Baptized.	Child's Christian Name.	Parents' Name.		Rank and Regiment.	Abode.	By whom Baptized.
			Christian.	Surname.			
51	June 3rd 1849	Anne	John & Anne	Hewitt	Col Serjeant 1 Royal	Linen Hall Bar	George Hare Chaplain
52	June 22nd 1849	Anna Mary Charlotte Corn McKay	Wm Fred & Frances Jane	Richards	Lieut 17 Lancers	Royal Bar	Geo Hare Chaplain
53	June 24th 1849	Ruth Jane	Joshua & Marion	Bolshaw	Serjt Major 17 Lancers	Royal Bar	G Hare Chaplain
54	June 24 1849	Maryanne	John & Anne	Crosbly	Private 48 Regt	Royal Bar	G Hare Chaplain
55	June 24 1849	Joseph	George & Mary	Robinson	Private 1 Royal	Linen Hall Bar	Geo Hare Chaplain
56	July 1st 1849	James	Robert & Margaret	Mitchel	Private 48 Regt	Royal Bar	S. Simpson Preb minister
57	July 1st 1849	Isabella	William & Fanny	Scott	Private 60 Rifles	Royal Bar	S. Simpson Preb minister
58	July 4th 1849	Arthur Brooke	George R & Grace	Smith	Surgeon 2 Regt Queens	Blackhall St	Geo Hare Chaplain
59	July 1849	Harriett Maryanne	William & Elizabeth	Toomey	Sorjeant 1 Royal	Linen Hall	Geo Hare Chaplain
60	July 8 1849	William	Mathew & Margaret	Gray	Private 48 Regt	Royal Bar	Geo Hare Chaplain

6. Church of Ireland baptisms in 1849 at the Military Church, Arbour Hill Barracks, Dublin.

7. Roman Catholic marriages in 1842/1843 at St. Peter & St. Paul's Church, Cork.

1675.

October 14.   Fortunata St. Nicholas, a foundling.
November 1.   John Tunstall.
,, 4.   Sarah daughter of Robert Alkin.
,, 11.   John son of Mr. John Twelves.
,, 24.   Gyles Cottrell.
December 4.   Samuel son of Mr. William Snell.
,, 5.   Susanna, daughter of Mr. Hugh Wormington.
February 25.   Hadassa, daughter of Mr. Joseph Saunders.
,, 8.   Vere Essex Williams son of Mr. Walter Welch.

1676.

March 10.   Adam son of Mr. Walter Welch.
,, 15.   Mr. Stephen Ludlow's daughter Susannah.
,, 15.   Mr. Ralph Moxon's son.
,, 15.   Mr. Ralph Moxon's daughter.
May 8.   Richard son of Mr. John Paggett.
,, 17.   Matthew Johnson.
June 9.   Mr. Booth's man.
,, 11.   Mr. Packenham's son.
,, 29.   Bridgett daughter of James Brumley.
August 28.   Jeremiah son of Richard Smith.
September 9.   Doctor Worsley's daughter.
October 5.   Elizabeth Robert, mother of Mr. Will Quinn.
November 21.   Robert, son of Mr. Thomas Packenham.
,, 22.   Jane daughter of Mr. James Fletcher.
,, 23.   Mr. Brice from Cornemarkett.
,, 27.   Mr. Burr from Mr. Butler's.
January 29.   Matthew son of Mr. John Warburton.
February 20.   James son of Sir Henry Inglesby.
,, 25.   Mr. Lord's wife from Castle Street.
,, 28.   Sarah wife of Anthony Cooley.

1677.

March 11.   Martha daughter of Mr. James Fletcher.
July 4.   Mr. Sherley in Back Lane.
September 22.   Anne the wife of Mr. Ralph Moxon.
,, 23.   Ann daughter of Mr. John Twelves.
November 23.   Mrs. Sarah Sanders daughter of Mr. Joseph Sanders.
January 2.   Christopher son of Mr. William Cooke.
,, 2.   Old William Jackson.
,, 4.   The wife of Councillor Price.
,, 13.   Nathaniel Harborne from the Ram.
,, 21.   The wife of Councillor James Grace.
,, 27.   Mrs. Accott from Swan Alley.
,, 28.   Tobias, son of Dr. Coghill.

8. Church of Ireland burials from 1675-1677 at St. Nicholas Within, Dublin.

A street in Cork, Ireland in 1927.

CHAPTER SIX
Wills and Administrations

Wills were proved and letters of administrations granted (in cases where there was no will) in Church of Ireland courts up to 1858. As was the case in England and Wales, the highest church court was a prerogative court, which, in Ireland, was the Prerogative Court of the Archbishop of Armagh. There were three other Irish archbishoprics (Cashel, Dublin and Tuam), but they didn't have prerogative courts.

Below this court were the consistory (or diocesan) courts of the various bishops, and also two 'peculiar' courts outside the bishops' control: Newry & Mourne (in County Down) and that of the Dean of Lismore (in County Waterford). There were no archdeaconry courts. As in England and Wales, when a testator left more than £5 worth of property in more than one diocese, his or her will had to be proved in the prerogative court. You can view maps showing the boundaries of the dioceses in Ireland's four ecclesiastical provinces free of charge at **www.origins.net/help/aboutio-wills-maps.aspx**.

In 1858, responsibility for proving wills was transferred to new civil probate registries, of which there was a Principal Probate Registry in Dublin and 11 district registries.

At the time of the explosion and fire in the Public Record Office of Ireland (PROI) in 1922, the PROI held all the wills and administrations proved in church courts, the records of the Principal Probate Registry up to 1904 and the original wills proved in the district registries up to 1899. Only 11 original prerogative wills (and copies of three more) and one diocesan will were saved, but fortunately the district registries had made copies of their wills before passing them to the Principal Registry.

The 11 prerogative wills were those of:

- *Elizabeth Clark, 1748;*
- *Elizabeth Clarke, 1768;*
- *James Stevenson, 1822;*
- *Robert Young, 1814;*
- *Robert Young, 1829;*
- *Thomas Young, 1835;*
- *Walter Young, 1812;*
- *William Young, 1813;*
- *William Young (Revd.), 1847;*
- *William Young, 1853;*
- *John Younge, 1834.*

The one diocesan will that wasn't destroyed was that of:

- *Margaret Burden, 1826*

in the 'peculiar' (exempt jurisdiction) of Newry and Mourne.

The three copies that survived were of the prerogative wills of:

- *Edward Cane, 1810;*
- *John Richard Irwin, 1836;*
- *Philip Perceval (Revd.), 1800.*

After the destruction of its will collection, the PROI immediately began to collect copies, transcripts, extracts and abstracts of the wills that had been destroyed. A card index of these was created, and this is now available at the National Archives of Ireland (NAI, the successor to the PROI), as well as on CD and online.

The NAI also holds a consolidated index of wills proved from 1858-77, and calendars of wills proved after 1877 (excluding Northern Ireland after 1918). The

Public Record Office of Northern Ireland (PRONI) holds all probated wills for Northern Ireland from 1900-1994.

Printed indexes

In addition, there is a printed index of the prerogative wills from 1536-1810 compiled by Sir Arthur Vicars (and published in 1897), abstracts of the wills from 1536-1800 created by Sir William Betham in the early 19th century, and pedigrees compiled by him from the abstracts.

A five-volume series of printed indexes of the diocesan wills up to 1800 (and in some areas up to 1858) was published between 1909 and 1920. The first three volumes were compiled by William P. W. Phillimore (the founder of the Phillimore publishing company), and after his death in 1913 the series was continued by Gertrude Thrift. It had been intended to cover the wills in all the dioceses and then publish similar indexes of the administrations, but the destruction of the PROI in 1922 put an end to the series.

The dioceses that had been covered are:

Volume	Diocese	Covering dates	Counties covered (main county first)
1	Ossory	1536-1800	Kilkenny, Laois
	Ferns	1601-1800	Wexford, Carlow, Wicklow
	Leighlin	1652-1800	Carlow, Laois, Kilkenny, Wexford, Wicklow
	Kildare	1661-1800	Kildare, Laois, Offaly, Wicklow
2	Cork & Ross	1548-1800	Cork, Kerry
	Cloyne	1621-1800	Cork, Limerick, Waterford
3	Cashel & Emly	1618-1800	Tipperary, Kilkenny, Limerick
	Waterford & Lismore	1645-1800	Waterford, Cork, Tipperary
	Killaloe & Kilfenora	1653-1800	Clare, Tipperary, Laois, Limerick
	Limerick	1615-1800	Limerick, Clare, Cork, Kerry
	Ardfert & Aghadoe	1690-1800	Kerry, Cork
4	Dromore	1678-1800	Down, Antrim, Armagh
	Newry & Mourne ('peculiar')	1727-1858	Down, Armagh
5	Derry	1615-1858	Derry/Londonderry, Antrim, Donegal, Tyrone
	Raphoe	1684-1858	Donegal

Wills and administrations online

At the subscription website Irish Origins **www.irishorigins.com** and at the subscription/pay-per-view site Findmypast Ireland **www.findmypast.ie**, you'll find an index of abstracts, extracts and copies of pre-1858 Irish probate records dating from 1484. More than half the records are wills, a quarter are administrations, and about 7% are marriage licence grants or bonds. Most of the records in the index (about 55%) are transcripts (many of them summaries), while 28% are abstracts or extracts, 10% original wills or grants and 7% full copies of wills.

In addition, both sites contains databases of entries in the Diocese of Dublin will and grant books from 1270-1858, Sir Arthur Vicars' index of the prerogative wills and the five-volume index of diocesan wills (see above).

There are several indexes and abstracts of Irish wills at the subscription site Ancestry.co.uk **www.ancestry.co.uk**, including the index to the prerogative wills, the five-volume diocesan wills index, 'A Guide to Copies and Abstracts of Irish Wills' by the Rev. Wallace Clare (published in 1930), 'Quaker Records, Dublin, Abstracts of Wills' by P. Beryl Eustace and Olive C. Goodbody (published in 1953) and 'Registry of Deeds, Dublin: Abstracts of Wills (1708-1785)' also by P. Beryl Eustace (published in the 1950s).

You can also view the 'Index to the Prerogative Wills of Ireland 1536-1810' at the Internet Archive **www.archive.org** free of charge. Family historian Ginni Swanton has put one of the five-volume diocesan indexes (for the Diocese of Cork & Ross) online at her free website **www.ginnisw.com/Indexes to Irish Wills/Thumb/Thumbs1.htm**.

Dr. Jane Lyons has transcribed the index to the wills of the Diocese of Ardagh and made it available free of charge at **www.from-ireland.net/genealogy/Will-Abstracts%3A-Ardagh-Diocese**. You'll also find that an index of wills proved in the Diocese of Raphoe and transcribed by Cathy Joint Labath is freely available at **http://freepages.genealogy.rootsweb.ancestry.com/~donegal/wills.htm**.

At the free website of the PRONI **www.proni.gov.uk**, you'll find indexed calendars of wills proved and administrations granted at the District Probate Registries of Armagh, Belfast and Londonderry from 1858-1919, part of 1921 and 1922-1943, with digitised images for the period 1858-1900.

The three registries indexed at this site had replaced the diocesan courts in 1858 and covered not only the six counties that became Northern Ireland in 1922, but also Counties Donegal, Louth and Monaghan in what is now the Irish Republic. There are even some wills in this index whose testators lived in County Cavan (also in the Irish Republic).

In addition, the PRONI's 'Name Search' index includes (among other records) more than 15,500 pre-1858 wills proved and administrations granted in the diocesan courts of what is now Northern Ireland and in the Prerogative Court of Armagh. Copies of some of the wills have survived, although none of the administration bonds has.

The National Archives of Ireland (NAI) has put annual alphabetical calendars of wills and administrations from 1923-1982 online for what is now the Republic of Ireland. Those for the period 1858-1922 are to be added later. You can browse these calendars through the website of the Council of Irish Genealogical Organisations (CIGO) **www.cigo.ie/httpwww.cigo.iewills.html**.

According to CIGO, the calendars from 1858-1920 are to be indexed and made fully searchable by FamilySearch. However, at the time of writing (August 2012), the contents of the FamilySearch wiki page on the subject had been 'removed until contract issues have been resolved'.

Among the members-only databases on the subscription-based Ulster Historical Foundation site **www.ancestryireland.com**, you'll find several indexes of wills proved in church courts up to 1858 and in civil district registries from 1858-1900.

Don't forget the pay-per-view Documents Online website of The [UK] National Archives **www.nationalarchives.gov.uk/documentsonline**, which includes more than 2,000 Irish wills proved in London up to 1858 at the Prerogative Court of Canterbury (the principal English church court). Searching is free of charge.

Similarly, at the Scottish Government's pay-per-view ScotlandsPeople site **www.scotlandspeople.gov.uk**, you'll find about 2,000 Irish wills that were confirmed by the Scottish courts. Searching the wills index is free of charge.

The library of the Society of Genealogists

In the SoG library, you'll find microfilms of Betham's will abstracts and pedigrees, and printed copies of Vicars' index of the prerogative wills. As well as the Phillimore/Thrift indexes of the diocesan wills, the society also holds printed indexes of wills proved in the dioceses of Ardagh (from 1695-1858), Clonfert (1663-1857), Connor (1818-1858), Down (1850-1858), Dublin (1457-1483 and 1536-1858), Killala & Achonry (1698-1858), Kilmore (1682-1857), Ossory (1848-1858).

In addition, there are printed indexes of administrations granted in the dioceses of Clonfert (from 1738-1857), Cloyne (1630-1857), Cork & Ross (1612-1858), Kildare (1770-1848), Killaloe & Kilfenora (1845) and Leighlin (1694-1845), as well as the 'peculiar' of Newry & Mourne (1811-1857).

The SoG holds a good deal of other testamentary material, including 18 typescript volumes of Irish wills from 1569-1858 abstracted by William Henry Welply, about 4,000 abstracts of Irish wills compiled by Lorna Rosbottom, three volumes of wills from 1708-1832 abstracted from the Registry of Deeds (see next chapter) by P. Beryl Eustace, and various other indexes and abstracts.

CHAPTER SEVEN
Registry of Deeds

The Registry of Deeds in Dublin is a vast treasure-house of Irish genealogical information that hasn't had as much prominence as it perhaps deserves. The registry began operating in 1708 to enable registration of Irish deeds and conveyances concerned with the transfer and holding of land, principally to prevent land falling into Roman Catholic hands. Although registration was voluntary, registered deeds were given priority treatment by the Irish Government.

Particularly in the Registry's first century, most of the 'grantors' (the people registering the deeds) belonged to the Protestant community who worshipped in the Church of Ireland. The 'grantees' (the other parties to the deed), on the other hand, might well be Catholics or Presbyterians, although rarely people with very small tenancies.

The deeds cover landowners ranging from the aristocracy and landed gentry to small farmers, as well as tradesmen and merchants, while servants may be witnesses to their signatures. Six main transaction types were registered (many of them under the description 'lease and release').

Sales, assignments and conveyances

Under this type of transaction, the grantee was to hold the property 'for ever'. Land that the courts had ordered to be sold would usually be covered

by a registered assignment, where the first party to the deed was the Master of the Court of Chancery or the Chief Remembrancer of the Court of Equity Exchequer.

Rent charges

These were deeds where a person granted someone else (such as a widowed mother or sister, or a creditor) an annual sum of money charged on certain property. Such rent charges could then be assigned to third or fourth parties.

Leases

This was the largest group of deeds, as most land in Ireland was held by lease for a period that could range from one to 999 years. Many leases were for a specified term (often 31 years) or three 'lives' (the lifetimes of three people), whose names and relationships are given, and sometimes their ages.

Mortgages

Mortgages were a way of raising ready money at a time when there was no stock market and an insecure banking system, and could be for a short term (such as a year or less) or an indefinite length of time. As was the case with leases, mortgages could be sold on for profit.

Marriage settlements

Many of these deeds were made by fathers to transfer sums of money to trustees in order to provide for their daughters after marriage, at a time when a married woman was not legally allowed to hold property in her own right. Also, a husband might make provision for an annuity to be paid to his wife, if she survived him.

Wills

From the opening of the Registry of Deeds until 1810 (but mainly up to 1785), many wills were registered, particularly if someone was being disinherited (and not mentioned in the will). These have been abstracted and printed, and are available at the Library of the Society of Genealogists and online (see previous chapter).

Memorials and indexes

Complete copies or detailed abstracts of the deeds being registered were transcribed as 'memorials' in large ledgers called Transcript Books (so large and heavy that they're known as 'tombstones').

The Registry of Deeds has two indexes: a Names Index and a Townlands Index (up to 1946). The Names Index contains an alphabetical list of 'grantors, with each entry also naming the 'grantee', while the Townlands Index will provide you with the names of the owners over the years. It's been estimated that there are about 1,000 volumes of the indexes alone.

You can view microfilm copies of the indexes and of the memorials themselves (both from 1708-1929) at LDS ('Mormon') Family History Centres. (The microfilms are also available to researchers at the Registry of Deeds itself and at the Public Record Office of Northern Ireland (PRONI) in Belfast.)

Online index

The Names and Townland Indexes aren't very easy to use, so Australian family historian Nick Reddan and a band of volunteers are creating an online index of abstracts from the memorials, which you can find at **http://freepages. genealogy.rootsweb.ancestry.com/~registryofdeeds**. There are about 35 transcripts of memorials at the site too.

Once you've found details of a memorial in the index, you can link to the website of the Republic of Ireland's Property Registration Authority to fill in an application form (Requisition for copy memorial/application form) at **www.landregistry.ie/ eng/Forms/Registry_of_Deeds_Forms**. There's a charge of €20 (about £17) for the copy memorial.

There are now (August 2012) more than 100,000 index records online for over 12,000 memorials of deeds, but as over half a million deeds had been registered by 1832 alone, it may take a very long time for volunteers to index it fully.

Registries of Deeds in Britain

There was no national Registry of Deeds for England, although five areas had local registries: the Bedford Level in Cambridgeshire (from 1663-1920), the West Riding of Yorkshire (from 1704-1970), the East Riding including Hull (from 1708-1974), Middlesex (from 1708-1940) and the North Riding (from 1736-1970).

In Scotland, land transfers were recorded in the Registers of Sasines, and other deeds in the Registers of Deeds of the Court of Session, commissary courts (up to 1809) and sheriff courts. The Perth Burgh Register of Deeds from 1566-1811 has been digitised, indexed and made available online at Ancestry.co.uk **www.ancestry.co.uk**.

CHAPTER EIGHT
Records of the Armed Forces

British Army

Other ranks

Although 26 of Ireland's 32 counties are now the Republic of Ireland, all of Ireland was part of the United Kingdom (UK) until the end of 1921, and many Irishmen and women from all parts of Ireland served in the UK's armed forces. Their records are included in the various collections held by The National Archives (TNA) in Kew, London, and many of those records are available online.

You'll find many detailed research guides to these records at **www.nationalarchives.gov.uk/records/atoz/default.htm**. The National Army Museum in London also has some useful information at **www.nam.ac.uk/research/family-history** that can help you trace your ancestors' military careers.

Officers and so-called 'other ranks' (privates and non-commissioned officers) in the British Army were recorded separately. You'll find the service records of other ranks for the period prior to the First World War in TNA's incomplete WO (War Office) 97 collection, which covers soldiers discharged to pension between 1760 and 1913.

These records have been digitised and indexed, and you can find them online at the subscription/pay-per-view site Findmypast **www.findmypast.co.uk**.

More service records for soldiers discharged to pension between 1787 and 1813 are held in the WO 121 collection. These records have not been digitised, but are indexed in the TNA Catalogue **www.nationalarchives.gov.uk/catalogue**, as are the WO 97 records. TNA is replacing its Catalogue with its new Discovery Catalogue **http://discovery.nationalarchives.gov.uk/SearchUI**.

Searching the Catalogue or Discovery will provide you with information such as:

'WO 121/161/113 - Patrick Walsh; born in Lickligh, Westmeath; served in 15th Foot Regiment, and 4th Royal Veteran Battalion; discharged [in 1804] aged 52, after 15 years 2 months of service; residence or place where pension paid stated in document.'

Using the reference number (in this case WO 121/161/113), you can order the record from TNA.

As well as soldiers' service records, TNA also holds other ranks' muster rolls and pay lists, which state enlistment dates, movements and discharge dates. The monthly or quarterly musters used for pay and accounting usually state age, place of enlistment and trade in a new recruit's first entry.

Most regiments' muster rolls and pay lists from 1730-1878 are in the series WO 12. Those for the Artillery, however, are in WO 10, WO 54 and WO 69, those for the Engineers in WO 11 and WO 54, for militia and volunteers in WO 13 and WO 68, and for the troops who were sent to the Scutari Depot during the Crimean War (from 1854-1856) in WO 14.

You'll find information from the WO 10, WO 11 and WO 12 collections in Findmypast's 1861 Worldwide Army Index.

As well as those in the WO 97 and WO 121 collections, you'll also find soldiers' pension records in WO 116, which contains disability pension admission books from 1715-1882. Length of service books from 1823-1913 are in the WO 117 collection.

You can download (currently free of charge) both the WO 116 and WO 117 records as a large block of unindexed 'digital microfilm' from TNA's Documents Online website **www.nationalarchives.gov.uk/documentsonline**. Documents Online is being phased out, but you can also find TNA's digital microfilm records at **www.nationalarchives.gov.uk/records/digital-microfilm.htm**.

Unfortunately, about 60% of other ranks' records for the First World War period were destroyed by bombing in 1940, including the records of soldiers who had enlisted before the war and were still serving or who had been recalled.

We have to be thankful that around two million soldiers' records either survived and are in the WO 363 collection (known as the 'burnt documents') or were reconstructed from pension records and are in the WO 364 collection (the 'unburnt documents').

You can search and view digitised images of both collections' records online at the subscription website Ancestry.co.uk **www.ancestry.co.uk**. Although these collections principally contain the service records of soldiers who served in the British Army during the First World War (together with records of any previous service), you'll also find the earlier service records of a few soldiers who didn't serve during the First World War.

Officers

You'll find printed records of officers of the British Army both in the official *Army List*, first published in 1740, and in the unofficial *Hart's Army List*, which was published between 1839 and 1915. You can view digitised copies of many of the lists at the subscription/pay-per-view site The Genealogist **www.thegenealogist.co.uk** and also free of charge at the Internet Archive **www.archive.org**.

In addition, both the TNA collections WO 65 (Printed Annual Army Lists) and WO 76 (Records of Officers' Service) can be downloaded (free of charge at present) as a large block of 'digital microfilm' from Documents Online.

Unfortunately, the main series of First World War officers' service records was destroyed in 1940, just as the other ranks' records had been. There is still a supplementary series of records for officers, however, although unfortunately some of the records had been destroyed by clerks. The officers' records contain attestation papers, service records and personal correspondence in some cases, but only the date of the officer's death in others.

There are nearly 140,000 service records in the WO 339 collection. These are records of officers who were either officers in the regular Army before the First World War, given a temporary commission, or commissioned into the Special Reserve of officers. The WO 374 collection contains almost 80,000 records of officers with a Territorial Army or temporary commission. Both the WO 339 and WO 374 records are indexed in TNA's Catalogue.

British Army records online

Ancestry.co.uk (A)
www.ancestry.co.uk

- British Army World War I Service Records 1914-1920 (TNA ref. WO 363)
- British Army World War I Pension Records 1914-1920 (WO 364)
- British Army World War I Medal Rolls Index Cards 1914-1920 (WO 372) (Also TNA)
- Royal Naval Division Casualties of the Great War 1914-1924
- Army War List 1893
- Military Campaign Medal and Award Rolls 1793-1949 (WO 100)
- Indian Army Quarterly List 1912
- Ireland, Casualties of World War I 1914-1918

Findmypast (FMP)
www.findmypast.co.uk (Many of these collections are also at Genes Reunited (GR) www.genesreunited.co.uk)

- British Army Service Records 1760-1913 (WO 97)
- Militia Service Records 1806-1915 (WO 96)
- 1861 Worldwide Army Index (WO 10, WO 11, WO 12)
- Army Deserters 1828-1840
- Other Army Lists and Roll Calls (includes Grenadier Guards 1656-1874; Peninsular Medal Roll 1793-1814; Waterloo Roll Call 1815; Army Lists 1787, 1798 and 1878; Hart's Army List 1840 and 1888; and Indian Army and Civil Service List 1873)
- Royal Fusiliers Collection 1863-1905
- Royal Naval Division 1914-1919
- Armed Forces Births 1761-2005, Marriages 1796-2005 and Deaths 1796-2005

Military Genealogy (MG)
www.military-genealogy.com

- Soldiers Died in the Great War 1914-1919 (Also A, FMP, GR)
- National Roll of the Great War 1914-1918 (Also A, FMP, TG)
- De Ruvigny's Roll of Honour 1914-1924 (Also A, FMP, TG)
- Citations of the Distinguished Conduct Medal 1914-1920 (Also A, FMP)
- Army Roll of Honour 1939-1945 (Also A, FMP)
- British Army Prisoners of War 1939-1945 (Also A, FMP)

- Casualties of the Boer War 1899-1902 (Also A, FMP, GR)
- Waterloo Medal Roll 1815 (Also A, FMP)

The Genealogist (TG)
www.thegenealogist.co.uk

- Bond of Sacrifice officers' roll of honour August 1914-June 1915
- British Roll of Honour 1914-1918
- Chatham, Plymouth and Portsmouth Memorial Register 1914-1921
- Various regimental histories

Commonwealth War Graves Commission
www.cwgc.org

- Debt of Honour Register (for First and Second World Wars)

The National Archives (TNA)
www.nationalarchives.gov.uk/records/our-online-records.htm

- Selected First World War and Army of Occupation War Diaries (WO 95)
- Women's (later Queen Mary's) Army Auxiliary Corps 1917-1920 (WO 398)
- British prisoners of war: interviews and reports (WO 161)
- Victoria Cross Registers (WO 98)
- Recommendations for Honours and Awards 1935 - 1990 (WO 373)

Other Boer War databases

- Roll of Honour **www.roll-of-honour.com/Databases/BoerDetailed/index.html**
- Cassus Belli **www.casus-belli.co.uk**

Royal Navy

Ratings

Ordinary seamen in the Royal Navy (who are the equivalent of 'other ranks' in the British Army), are known as 'ratings'. Continuous Service Engagement Books for ratings who joined the Navy from 1853-1872 are in TNA's collection ADM (Admiralty) 139. You'll find ratings who joined up from 1873-1923 in the Register of Seamen's Services in ADM 188. You can search both collections at Documents Online (see overleaf).

TNA's Trafalgar Ancestors database (of over 8,000 mainly Royal Navy and Royal Marine personnel) may contain one of your ancestors who fought with Lord Nelson at the Battle of Trafalgar in 1805. You'll find the database at **www.nationalarchives. gov.uk/trafalgarancestors**.

Officers

Registers of officers' services from 1756-1966 (although most cover the period 1840-1920) are in the series ADM 196. The records have been digitised and can be viewed at Documents Online (see below).

If you're looking for information on officers' service prior to 1840, you should look in the unofficial *Steele's Navy List* (published from 1782), the official *Navy List* (published quarterly from 1814), and the unofficial *New Navy List* which contains short biographies (published from 1841-1856). Digitised copies of the various lists are online at The Genealogist and at the Internet Archive.

Royal Navy records online

The National Archives (TNA)

- Register of Seamen's Services 1853-1923 (ADM 139, ADM 188)
- Royal Naval Officers' Service Records 1756-1917 (ADM 196)
- Royal Naval Officers' Service Record Cards and Files 1880-1960 (ADM 340)
- Royal Naval Division Service Records 1914-1919 (ADM 339)
- Royal Naval Volunteer Reserve, First World War (ADM 337)
- Royal Naval Reserve Service Records 1860-1908 (BT 164)
- Women's Royal Naval Service 1917-1919 (ADM 318, ADM 336)
- Wills of Royal Naval Seamen 1786-1882 (ADM 48)

Ancestry.co.uk (A)

- British Naval Biographical Dictionary 1849
- Commissioned Sea Officers of the Royal Navy 1660-1815
- Royal Navy and Royal Marine War Graves Roll 1914-1919
- Navy Medal and Award Rolls 1793-1972

Findmypast (FMP)

- Royal Naval Officers 1914-1920 (ADM 171/89-93, ADM 171/139)

Military Genealogy (MG)

Naval Casualties 1914-1919 (Also FMP, and similar to Ancestry's Royal Naval Division Casualties)

Royal Air Force

Airmen

The Royal Air Force (RAF) came into being on 1 April 1918, when the Royal Flying Corps (RFC, an Army unit set up in 1912) was combined with the Royal Naval Air Service (RNAS, founded in 1914), and began taking on new recruits.

'Airmen' are the RAF equivalent of the Army's 'other ranks'. You'll find the RFC service records of airmen who died or were discharged before the formation of the RAF in the WO 363 or 364 collections (online at Ancestry.co.uk), while the equivalent RNAS service records are in ADM 188 (at Documents Online).

The records of airmen who were still serving in the RFC or RNAS when the RAF was created were transferred to the new service. The series AIR 79 contains these records, together with those of airmen who joined up after the creation of the RAF, while you'll find an index in AIR 78. Although airmen's records have not yet been made available online, you can search AIR 79 using the TNA Catalogue or Discovery.

Officers

The service records of RAF and RFC officers are in the TNA collection AIR 76, which has been digitised and is available at Documents Online. This collection also holds records of RNAS officers still serving when the RAF was founded. The records of RNAS officers who had died or been discharged before 1918, however, are in TNA's ADM 273 collection, which you can search in the Catalogue. The official *Air Force List* from March 1919 also has information on RAF officers, and you can find the 1939 list online at The Genealogist.

Royal Air Force records online

The National Archives (TNA)

- RAF Officers' Service Records 1918-1919 (AIR 76)
- WRAF Service Records 1918-1920 (AIR 80)
- Air Combat Reports, Second World War (AIR 50)

Royal Marines

Other ranks

The Royal Marines (RM) were first raised in 1664, and are 'sea soldiers' who are neither part of the British Army nor of the Royal Navy. RM attestation forms (enlistment and discharge papers) from 1790-1925 are held by TNA in its ADM 157 collection, which is being indexed in the TNA Catalogue.

RM description books from 1755-1940 are in ADM 158, and service records from 1842-1936 in ADM 159. The service records have been digitised and indexed, and are online at Documents Online.

The Royal Marines' main divisions were based in Chatham (in Kent), Portsmouth (Hampshire), Plymouth (Devon) and from 1805-69 Woolwich (Kent, and now the London Borough of Greenwich). The RM Artillery, RM Engineers and RM Labour Corps (in Chatham and Deal) are also included in the RM records.

Officers

You'll find Royal Marines' officers listed in the *Army List* (from 1740), the *Navy List* (from 1797), *Hart's Army List* and the *New Navy List* (from 1840). Many editions of these lists are online at the Internet Archive. From 1793 onwards, you can find RM officers' service records with those of Royal Navy officers in ADM 196 collection, which is available at Documents Online.

Royal Marines' records online

The National Archives (TNA)

- Royal Marines Registers of Service 1842-1936 (ADM 159)
- Selected Plymouth Attestations 1805-1848 (ADM 157/140)

Ancestry.co.uk (A)

- Royal Navy and Royal Marine War Graves Roll 1914-1919

Findmypast (FMP)

- Royal Marine Medal Roll 1914-1920 (ADM 171/167-171, ADM 171/92, ADM 171/139)

How to apply for a post-First World War service record

You'll find the records of British Army other ranks who were still serving in the Army after 1920, and officers still serving after 31 March 1922, at the Ministry of Defence (MOD, the successor to the War Office).

The MOD also holds the records of ratings who joined the Royal Navy after 1923 (and those already in the Navy who served beyond 1928), as well as those of officers who served after the First World War.

Records of airmen whose service number is higher than 329000 (and also of those whose number is lower, but served in the RAF during the Second World War) are held by the MOD, as are those of officers still serving after 1920.

The Ministry also has records of Royal Marines other ranks who enlisted after 1925, as well as the records of officers appointed after that year.

The MOD can supply you with information from the record of someone who served in the forces - provided that their service record has not yet been made available at TNA. You are required to supply the person's death certificate and to pay a fee of £30. You'll find a link to the MOD's website (which has full information and downloadable application forms) at **www.veterans-uk.info/service_records/service_records.html**

1818 Pinkerton Map of Ireland, Geographicus.

58

CHAPTER NINE
Maps

I t's always good to be able to see exactly where your ancestors lived, and the maps mentioned in this chapter - which can all be viewed free of charge - should help you to do that.

The Republic of Ireland's Ordnance Survey has made a map viewer available online at **http://maps.osi.ie/publicviewer**. At that site, you can click on a 1:2,500,000 map of Ireland to increase the scale to 1:500,000, and keep clicking until you eventually reach a scale of 1:2,000.

You can change the map view to show historic details either in colour or black and white from a six inches to the mile map (dating from 1837-1842), or in black and white from a 25 inches to the mile map (dating from 1888-1913). The colour maps highlight the boundaries of townlands (parish sub-divisions).

Modern administrative maps can be downloaded from the Ordnance Survey of Northern Ireland's map shop **http://maps.osni.gov.uk/CMSPages/ admin_boundaries.aspx**. Maps from 1974, 1984 and 1992 are available showing the 26 modern local government districts in Northern Ireland (which replaced the six counties administratively in 1973). The 1974 maps also show townland boundaries.

As mentioned in Chapter 4, at **www.askaboutireland.ie/griffith-valuation**, the website Ask About Ireland also has maps showing the division of parishes into townlands. These are further sub-divided into the lots listed in Griffith's Valuation.

The MAPCO website **http://mapco.net** contains William Wilson's plan of Dublin in 1798, with an 1836 map, an 1846 panoramic view and an 1895 plan of the city set to follow.

You'll find a map showing Irish civil registration districts at **www.connorsgenealogy.com/wpe24.jpg**, while Irish professional genealogist John Grenham's website has maps showing the location of both civil parishes **www.irishtimes.com/ancestor/browse/counties/civilmaps** and Roman Catholic parishes **www.irishtimes.com/ancestor/browse/counties/rcmaps**.

The Leitrim-Roscommon Genealogy website has a map page at **www.leitrim-roscommon.com/LR_maps.html** with maps showing the Roman Catholic parishes, civil parishes, baronies (similar to hundreds or wapentakes in England) and Poor Law Union areas in the two counties. You'll also find maps showing the townlands within many of the Roman Catholic and civil parishes.

Dennis Walsh's website Irish History in Maps **www.rootsweb.ancestry.com/~irlkik/ihm** has 24 maps depicting Irish history from the ice ages through the Viking settlement, Norman invasion, English and Scottish plantations, up to the Great Famine in the 1840s. In addition, the site has a number of surname lists.

Since 2004, University College Cork has been developing an Atlas of Irish Names at **www.ucc.ie/research/atlas**. This is part of a project to establish the origins of Irish surnames, establish ethnic diversity (in particular, the Norse contribution) and analyse the changing distribution of surnames since the 'plantations' in the 17th century and upheavals in the late 19th century.

The project has abstracted and mapped data for 150 surnames from Griffith's Valuation and has produced several online maps showing the distribution of surnames by civil parish. So far (August 2012), there are maps for the surnames Brennan, Carney, Collins, Connolly, Foley, Kenny, Kerr, King, Moran and Quinn. In the longer term, the project intends to produce an atlas with about 300 surname distribution maps.

CHAPTER TEN
Newspapers

Newspapers anywhere are always a good source of all sorts of little stories about people that you aren't likely to find elsewhere. In addition, for Ireland, they can also help to supply some of the genealogical information that would otherwise be missing, such as the birth, marriage and death announcements that began to appear around 1750.

The earliest Irish newspapers were published in Dublin, including the *Dublin Evening Post* (from 1719), *Faulkner's Dublin Journal* (from 1725), the *Freeman's Journal* (from 1763) and the *Dublin Hibernian Journal* (from 1771). These papers were joined in the early 19th century by the *Dublin Morning Post, Dublin Evening Herald* and *Dublin Evening Mail.*

The Dublin newspapers carried marriage and death notices from the mid-1750s, including abbreviated versions of those that had appeared in Irish provincial papers a week or so earlier. These notices decreased in the early years of the 19th century, particularly for Dublin itself, although elsewhere in Ireland their numbers increased.

One of the earliest Irish provincial newspapers was the *Belfast Newsletter* (from 1737). This was followed by the *Belfast Evening Post* (founded as the *Belfast Mercury* in 1783), the *Northern Star* (from 1792), the *Belfast*

Commercial Chronicle (from 1805), *Belfast Mercantile Register* (from 1822), the *Northern Whig* (from 1824), the *Guardian* (from 1827) and the *Banner of Ulster* (from 1842).

Irish newspapers online

At the Irish Times Digital Archive subscription website **www.irishtimes.com/ search/index.htm**, you can view and download digitised pages of the *Irish Times* from 1859 to the present. Many editorials and other articles are available to read and download free of charge.

Digital images of more than two million copies of 21 Irish regional and national newspapers from 1763 to the present (including the *Freeman's Journal*, *Irish Independent* (from 1905) and *Sunday Independent* (from 1906)) can be viewed and downloaded at the Irish Newspaper Archives subscription site **www.irishnewsarchive.com**.

The British Library (BL) has copies of many Irish newspapers (including some of those published in Belfast, Carlow, Castlebar, Clonmel, Cork, Drogheda, Dublin, Enniskillen, Galway, Kilkenny, Limerick, Derry/Londonderry, Roscommon, Sligo, Strabane, Tralee, Waterford and Wexford). Some of these newspapers have already been made available at the BL's subscription-based British Newspaper Archive **www.britishnewspaperarchive.co.uk** and more will be added during the coming years.

Free websites include the Ireland Old News site **www.irelandoldnews.com**, where you can view transcriptions taken from various 18th and 19th century Irish newspapers. In addition, the site has an index of about 54,500 death notices for people who were born in or died in Ireland.

Another free site is Australian family historian Nick Reddan's Index **http://members.pcug.org.au/~nickred/newspaper/search_index.html**, which has many extracts taken from 16 Irish newspapers from the period 1720-1865.

Dr. John C. Greene of the Department of English at the University of Louisiana, Lafayette and his many helpers have made an index to the *Belfast Newsletter* from 1737-1800 available free of charge at **www.ucs.louisiana.edu/bnl**. Although the run of the newspaper from 1754-1800 is nearly complete, few of the earlier issues has survived.

The Belfast Gazette (like those for London and Edinburgh) has been one of the 'official newspapers of record' for the United Kingdom since 7 June 1921, and contains information from many Government departments. Northern Ireland personal insolvencies, as well as New Year and Queen's Birthday Honours lists, are published in the *Gazette* and its supplements. Most issues can be searched and viewed free of charge at **www.belfast-gazette.co.uk**.

Prior to the partition of Ireland, the UK's official Irish newspaper was *The Dublin Gazette*, which had been published since 1706 and has been known as *Iris Oifigiúil* (Irish State News) since 31 January 1922. You can search and view an archive of the publication (from 2002 onwards) at **www.irisoifigiuil.ie**.

Emigrants Leave Ireland, 1868, by Henry Doyle.

64

CHAPTER ELEVEN
Surnames and Migration

In 1894, Robert Matheson, Assistant Register-General of Marriages, Births and Deaths in Ireland, published a *Special Report on Surnames in Ireland, with Notes as to Numerical Strength, Derivation, Ethnology and Distribution* as an appendix to the Registrar-General's 29th annual report.

Matheson listed the hundred most common surnames in Ireland from the births index of 1890, estimated numbers of people with those names, and the 10-20 most common surnames in each county (more than 20 in Counties Cork, Dublin and Louth). The estimated total population of Ireland in 1890 was about 4.7 million.

Here are the first 20 names from Matheson's list, together with estimated numbers:

Position	Surname	Est. nos.	Counties where this is the most common surname
1	Murphy	62,600	Armagh, Carlow and Wexford
2	Kelly	55,900	Galway, Kildare, Leitrim, Offaly and Roscommon
3	Sullivan	43,600	Cork and Kerry
4	Walsh	41,700	Mayo
5	Smith	33,700	Antrim
6	O'Brien	33,400	
7	Byrne	33,300	Dublin, Louth and Wicklow
8	Ryan	32,000	Limerick and Tipperary
9	Connor	31,200	
10	O'Neill	29,100	
11	Reilly	29,000	Cavan, Longford and Meath
12	Doyle	23,000	
13	McCarthy	22,300	
14	Gallagher	21,800	Donegal
15	Doherty	20,800	Derry/Londonderry

Position	Surname	Est. nos.	Counties where this is the most common surname
16	Kennedy	19,900	
17	Lynch	19,800	Westmeath
18	Murray	19,600	
19	Quinn	18,200	Tyrone
20	Moore	17,700	

The following additional surnames were the most common in the remaining counties: Brennan (in Counties Kilkenny and Sligo, and no. 28 nationally), Dunne (in County Laois, and 27 nationally), McMahon (in County Clare, and 64 nationally), Power (in County Waterford, and 54 nationally), Thompson (in County Down, and 42 nationally), Maguire (in County Fermanagh, and 39 nationally) and Duffy (in County Monaghan, and 45 nationally).

In addition, Matheson listed all surnames with five entries or more in the 1890 birth indexes, showing the total number registered, the numbers registered in the provinces of Leinster, Munster, Ulster and Connaught (or Connacht), as well as naming the counties in which the names were mainly found.

You can view and download Matheson's *Special Report* free of charge at the Internet Archive **www.archive.org** and at Google Books **http://books.google.co.uk**.

Irish clans

Matheson pointed out that the majority of Ireland's most common names had a Celtic (i.e. Gaelic) origin, and that many of these names retained the prefixes 'O' (grandson of) and Mac (son of). He devoted several pages to what he called the 'Ancient Celtic Families, with the counties in which they were located' of which about 120 had surnames with the prefix 'Mac' and 420 with the prefix 'O'.

You'll find brief information on the origins of most Irish surnames in Edward MacLysaght's *The Surnames of Ireland*, while John Grenham's *Clans and Families of Ireland: The Heritage and Heraldry of Irish Clans and Families* covers the history of the Irish people, and focuses on the 200 commonest surnames many with an illustration of the family head's coat of arms.

Peter Beresford Ellis's *Erin's Blood Royal: The Gaelic Noble Dynasties of Ireland* contains the histories of 20 families of the old Gaelic aristocracy from their beginnings down to the present day. Although most of Ireland is a republic, the Chief Herald of Ireland gives their heads 'courtesy recognition' as chiefs.

Ellis names the families as those of:

In Munster: The MacCarthy Mór, Prince of Desmond; the O'Callaghan; the O'Carroll of Ely; the O'Donoghue of the Glens; the O'Donovan; the O'Long; the MacGillycuddy of the Reeks; the O'Brien and the O'Grady.

In Connacht: The O'Connor Don, Prince of Thomond; the O'Kelly of Gallagh and Tycooly; the MacDermot, Prince of Coolavin; and the O'Ruairc, Prince of Breifne.

In Ulster: The O'Neill Mór, Prince of Tyrone; the O'Neill, Prince of Clanaboy; the O'Dogherty of Inishowen; the O'Donel, Prince of Tirconnell; and the Maguire, Prince of Fermanagh.

In Leinster: The MacMorrough Kavanagh, Prince of Leinster; the O'Morchoe; and the Fox.

Immigration to Ireland

Matheson gives examples of surnames found in Ireland that were brought to Ireland by the various peoples who settled there: names of Danish/Norwegian, Anglo-Norman, English, Cornish, Welsh, Scots, Huguenot, German Palatine and Jewish origin.

In 1366, Englishmen who had settled in Ireland (known later as the Anglo-Irish) were instructed to 'be named by an English name, leaving off entirely the manner of naming used by the Irish'. The manner referred to was the use of patronymics, whereby the person's last name could change each generation, according to the name of his or her father or grandfather.

Almost 100 years later, this was extended to Irishmen living in the counties of the Pale (the area under direct English control), who were told to adopt an English surname, which could be the name of a town, a colour or an occupation.

In the mid-16th century, large English settlements known as 'plantations' were established in King's and Queen's Counties (now known as Offaly and Laois or Leix), as well as in parts of Counties Cork, Kerry, Limerick, Tipperary and Waterford. By 1641, an estimated 22,000 settlers had arrived.

In the north, Scottish settlers arrived in County Antrim and the Ards area of County Down around the same time. In 1609, Counties Armagh, Cavan, Coleraine (which was enlarged as County Londonderry, now also known as County Derry), Donegal,

Fermanagh and Tyrone were planted with Scots (about two thirds of the settlers, and mainly Presbyterian) and English (one third, and mainly Anglican). By 1641, an estimated 15,000 had arrived.

At the end of the 17th century, around 10,000 French Protestants (Huguenots) arrived in Ireland, with many settling in what is now County Laois. They were followed in the early 18th century by about 3,000 German Protestants (Palatines) from what is now the state of Rheinland-Pfalz (Rhineland-Palatinate). By this time, about 25% of the population of Ireland was Protestant, descended from the settlers who had arrived in the previous 200 years.

Emigration from Ireland

As well as immigration to Ireland, there was much emigration from the island, with about eight million people leaving in the century after 1815. Before the Great Famine of the mid to late 1840s, most of the emigration was to Canada, and from then until the start of the First World War the United States was the emigrants' main choice.

After that war, most movement from Ireland was across the Irish Sea. There had been much migration from Ireland to Britain during the 19th century too, but there was no official record of the names or numbers of Irishmen and women arriving in Britain, as they were regarded as simply moving from one part of the United Kingdom to another.

You can find them in the British census returns, although in most cases, there's no indication of where they came from, other than simply 'Ireland' (as that was all that was officially required). Sometimes more information was given, however, so it's a good idea to look at the returns for all the census years and for all the members of the family. You may be lucky.

Approximate numbers of people living in Britain who specified 'Ireland' as their birthplace, according to the census databases at the subscription website Ancestry.co.uk **www.ancestry.co.uk**, were:

Year	England	Wales	Scotland
1841	275,821	7,607	126,287
1851	488,501	22,332	191,937
1861	566,035	25,815	196,865
1871	555,697	28,097	203,038
1881	536,796	23,727	211,952

1891	443,543	20,521	194,392
1901	415,553	23,693	203,739
1911	319,711	14,761	---

Clan and family information online

Ancestry.co.uk holds the following databases:

- Visitation of Ireland (genealogies of families with coats of arms) 1897;
- Irish pedigrees 1923;
- Irish Landed Gentry 1887;
- Irish names and surnames 1923;
- Burke's Commoners of Great Britain and Ireland 1837/1838;
- Burke's Landed Gentry of Great Britain and Ireland 1855 (a newer edition of the above);
- Burke's Extinct and Dormant Baronetcies of England, Ireland and Scotland 1841;
- Burke's Peerage and Baronetage (Vol. 2, L-Z) 1865;
- The Complete Peerage of England, Scotland, Ireland, Great Britain and the United Kingdom 1910-1916;
- Debrett's Peerage of England, Scotland and Ireland 1808.

The subscription/pay-per-view website Findmypast Ireland **www.findmypast.ie** has these databases:

- Tipperary clans archive (indexes and transcripts of Irish newspapers, monumental inscriptions and various other publications);
- Alumni Dublinenses 1924 (provosts, professors, graduates and students of Trinity College, Dublin);
- Burke's Landed Gentry of Ireland 1899.

Many of the peerage and landed gentry volumes listed above can be viewed and downloaded free of charge at the Internet Archive and Google Books.

The library of the Society of Genealogists

The Society has a number of books on immigration to Ireland, in particular about Huguenot, Palatine, Scottish and Jewish arrivals. There are also many volumes on Irish emigration, particularly to the USA, Canada, Australia and New Zealand. In addition, the SoG has copies of many of the peerage and landed gentry volumes listed above.

Narrow rural road in hilly landscape in Ireland.

CHAPTER TWELVE
Background Information

I f you want to know more about *how* your ancestors lived, rather than just having a list of names and dates, then you need to find out about the area *where* they lived. There are various old books that can help you, some of which cover individual parishes and others whole counties. Digitised copies of some of the publications described below are available online free of charge at the Internet Archive **www.archive.org** and Google Books **http://books.google.co.uk**.

Statistical Account of Ireland

In 1790, Sir John Sinclair, the MP for Caithness in the north of Scotland, persuaded the 938 ministers of the Church of Scotland to write about their parishes for a *Statistical Account of Scotland*. The individual accounts are descriptions of the landscape, the crops, and the fish in the rivers and the sea. They also cover the price of food and clothing, how many people lived in the parish, their superstitions and what language they spoke.

Inspired by Sir John's work in Scotland, Edward Ledwich, vicar of Aghaboe in County Laois (at that time known as Queen's County), wrote a 96-page account of the parish, which was published in 1796.

Nearly 20 years later, William Shaw Mason began to edit a *Statistical Account of Ireland*, in which many more parish accounts were written by local clergymen on the model of Sir John Sinclair's Scottish accounts. Three volumes (covering a total of 79 out of nearly 1,200 parishes in Ireland) were published between 1814 and 1819, but unfortunately, no more appeared after that.

Some of the comments in the Irish accounts would today be considered politically incorrect and simply reinforcing stereotypes. For instance, in the account for Kilgeriff, County Cork, (in Mason's second volume) the Revd. Horatio Townsend writes:

> 'The common Irish are naturally shrewd, but very ignorant, and deficient in mental culture, from the barbarous tongue in which they converse, which operates as an effectual bar to any kind of literary attainment; like all of a similar description, they are addicted to pilfering, and have very imperfect notions of moral rectitude. They are, however, generally quiet and industrious, except when whiskey is cheap. The language of the common Roman Catholic peasantry is Irish; Protestants of the lower order speak both English and Irish; in town, English is frequently spoken by both.'

Ordnance Survey Memoirs

In the 1830s, the Ordnance Survey, which publishes maps and plans, compiled Irish parish-based accounts known as Memoirs to accompany them. Only the northern counties of Ireland were covered before the scheme was dropped and only one parish survey (Templemore in County Derry/Londonderry) was published at the time. It was not until 1993 that all 40 remaining volumes of the *Ordnance Survey Memoirs* were published by the Institute of Irish Studies at the Queen's University of Belfast (QUB), in conjunction with the Royal Irish Academy in Dublin.

You can find an online index of parishes covered at the QUB's Irish Studies Gateway **www.qub.ac.uk/schools/IrishStudiesGateway/Research/PastResearch/Ordinan ceSurveyMemoirs** (I notice that they've put an 'i' into the word 'Ordnance' in the web address). The main counties covered are Antrim (14 volumes), Armagh (one vol.), Derry/Londonderry (14 vols.), Donegal (two vols.), Down (four vols.), Fermanagh (two vols.) and Tyrone (four vols.). In addition, a single volume covers parts of Counties Cavan, Leitrim, Louth, Monaghan and Sligo.

County-based publications

In his two-volume work *An Account of Ireland Statistical and Political* (which covers the country generally), published in 1812, Edward Wakefield lists the county publications of the Dublin Society (the Royal Dublin Society from 1820). Many of the society's statistical surveys (plus a few published later) are available to read online (or download) at the Internet Archive or Google Books websites:

County	Year of publication	Author
Antrim	1812	Revd. John Dubourdieu
Armagh	1804	Sir Charles Coote
Cavan	1802	Sir Charles Coote
Clare	1808	Hely Dutton
Cork	1810	Revd. Horatio Townsend
Donegal	1802	Dr. James McParlan
Down	1802	Revd. John Dubourdieu
Dublin	1801	Joseph Archer
Dublin (observations on the Archer volume)	1802	Hely Dutton
Galway	1824	Hely Dutton
Kildare	1807	Thomas James Rawson
King's County (Offaly)	1801	Sir Charles Coote
Mayo	1802	Dr. James McParlan
Meath	1802	Robert Thompson
Monaghan	1801	Sir Charles Coote
Queen's County (Laois)	1801	Sir Charles Coote
Roscommon	1832	Isaac Weld
Sligo	1802	Dr. James McParlan
Tyrone	1802	John McEvoy
Wexford	1807	Robert Fraser

Also available online is a revised version of George Vaughan Sampson's Dublin Society County of Londonderry volume, which was issued in 1814 by another publisher.

In the *Statistical Survey of the County of Tyrone*, John McEvoy writes:

'The size of farms differs very much throughout the county; mountainous farms are generally of great extent, and are seldom divided in themselves, or even from each other.

It is common for several persons to be concerned in one townland, in the way of common, or run-dale, as it is usually called; each person to pay a proportion of rent, suppose a fourth or fifth, as the case may be; this determines the quantity of land each is to cultivate for his own part; but the cattle run in common, and the number, to the share of each person, is also determined by his proportion of the rent.

This system is attended with many inconveniencies to the land-holder, and is the greatest impediment to improvements. There is no emulation for draining, enclosing, liming or carrying into execution any permanent improvements, as long as this system exists, since none of the party have any division, which may be properly called their own. If one person should be disposed to improve, another, or perhaps the whole party, may be averse to it, and thus the business of improving the farm is dropped altogether.

The low lands of Newtown-Stewart and Aughentaine, the property of Lord Mountjoy, are in general well divided, and in many parts well planted with thorn quicks, and timber trees. Farms vary in size from five to fifty acres, and they are much greater in the mountainous parts.'

Gazetteers

Gazetteers describe localities, sometimes in great detail, particularly in the case of large towns and cities. Samuel Lewis's *Topographical Dictionary of Ireland* (published in 1837) is online at the free Library Ireland site **www.libraryireland.com**.

Under 'Dublin, City of', you'll find the following information about the associations for the relief and protection of orphans and destitute children:

The Foundling Hospital, a very extensive establishment in James Street, for the reception of infants of this description from all parts of Ireland, for many years afforded an asylum to 2,000 deserted children within its walls, and to nearly 5,000 who were kept at nurse in the country till of age to be admitted into the central establishment; these children were clothed, maintained, educated, and apprenticed from the funds of the hospital, which were assisted by annual parliamentary grants of from £20,000 to £30,000.

The internal departments were wholly closed by order of government on the 31st of March, 1835, and all the children who are not apprenticed, amounting to 2,541, are at present settled with nurses in the country. There are also about 2,800 apprentices serving their time as servants and to trades, who are still under the superintendence of the governors.

Directories

Also good for parish descriptions and histories are directories, which list private citizens (landowners, etc.) and tradesmen. Transcriptions of more than 40 Irish directories and almanacs (both national and local) dating from 1783-1924 are online at Findmypast Ireland **www.findmypast.ie**.

You can also search nearly 30 19th century directories covering what has since become Northern Ireland at the Public Record Office of Northern Ireland website **www.proni.gov.uk/index/search_the_archives/street_directories.htm**. Many other digitised copies of directories are available at the Internet Archive and Google Books.

At the Library Ireland site, you'll find many extracts from *Thom's Irish Almanac and Official Directory for the Year 1862*, including this description of Belfast's industries:

'Belfast is the nucleus of the Irish linen manufacture, and the country spinners and manufacturers meet those of the town on Fridays in the Commercial Buildings, which is the public Exchange. This trade is now in a flourishing condition and rapidly increasing.

There are in the town and vicinity 33 mills, and in all Ireland 76, numbering 506,000 spindles. Those in the town are all worked by steam power, and employ 32,000 hands. There are 5 cotton spinning factories in or near the town, containing 90,000 spindles.

The other chief branches of industry are linen and cotton weaving, iron founding on an extensive scale, and bleaching. There are also print works, flour mills, chemical works, oil mills, alabaster and barilla mills, saw mills, breweries, distilleries, several tan yards, a patent felt manufactory, flax-steeping works, &c, 5 large ship yards, with 2 patent slips, and yards for manufacturing ropes and sail-cloth.

Fairs are held on the first Wednesday of each month; Markets on Fridays, besides daily markets for domestic purposes.

The inland trade is carried on by the Lagan navigation, which connects the town with Lough Neagh, the Ulster Canal, which connects Lough Neagh with Enniskillen, and by the Ulster, Ballymena, and County Down Railways, which connect the town with the Counties of Antrim, Down, Armagh, Tyrone, and Derry; a railroad from the Cave Hill, 3 miles from Belfast, conveys limestone to the quays.

The termini of the Ulster, Ballymena, and County Down railways are handsome structures. The Ulster Railway communicates with Dublin at Portadown station, where it joins the Dublin and Belfast Junction Line.'

The library of the Society of Genealogists

The Society's library has copies of the 40 volumes of the *Ordnance Survey Memoirs* that were published in the late 20th century, Samuel Lewis's *Topographical Dictionary of Ireland* (in two volumes), many lists and directories covering all of Ireland as well as for many individual counties (particularly Counties Antrim, Cork and Dublin).

CHAPTER THIRTEEN
Monumental Inscriptions

The inscriptions on gravestones and on tablets inside and outside churches are helpful wherever your ancestors lived, but with so many Irish church registers either destroyed or late in starting, monumental inscriptions (MIs) are particularly useful.

After the Reformation in the 16th century, the Christian church became divided between the old Roman Catholic and the new Protestant denominations. In Ireland, most of the original Catholic churches were taken over at that time by the (Protestant) Church of Ireland (CoI), but their graveyards continued to be used for the burial of members of both denominations.

The CoI was (and still is) an Anglican church, but most of the Scots who arrived in the north of Ireland in the 17th century were Protestant Presbyterians (who have no bishops or archbishops). In places where a new CoI church was built, its graveyard would tend to be used for the burial of any Protestants, but not of Catholics.

Once Presbyterianism became established as a separate denomination in Ireland in the late 17th century, members of its congregations would usually be buried in an old parish graveyard, rather than that of a new CoI church. By the late 18th and early 19th century, new Presbyterian and Catholic

graveyards began to be laid out, as well as those of Moravians and Quakers (the Religious Society of Friends).

Many MIs have been transcribed and made available online, while the Society of Genealogists' Library holds copies of many printed booklets of MI transcriptions.

Monumental inscriptions online

You can search all the websites below free of charge, although some of the sites do make a charge for access to the full inscription.

The pay-per-view site Irish World **www.irish-world.com/gravestones** has a database of more than 400,000 MIs from gravestones in the north of Ireland. The database covers graveyards in Counties Antrim, Armagh, Derry/Londonderry, Donegal, Down, Fermanagh, Louth, Monaghan and Tyrone.

The Ulster Historical Foundation (UHF) has published many MIs from Counties Antrim and Down both in booklet form and on sets of microfiche. These MIs are also available online at the pay-per-view site History from Headstones **www.historyfromheadstones.com**. There you can search a database of more than 50,000 MIs from more than 800 graveyards in Counties Antrim, Armagh, Derry/Londonderry, Down, Fermanagh and Tyrone. Members of the UHF's Ulster Genealogical and Historical Guild (see Chapter 16) have unlimited access to the History from Headstones database via the members' area of the UHF website Ancestry Ireland **www.ancestryireland.com**.

The free American website Ancestors at Rest has Irish pages at **http://ancestorsatrest.com/ireland_genealogy.shtml** that include many transcriptions of MIs from graveyards in Counties Wicklow, Offaly, Meath and Louth, as well as other Irish records. The site also contains an interesting series of articles on the history of Irish headstones.

You'll also find Irish MI transcriptions at the free US site Interment.net **www.interment.net** under both 'Republic of Ireland' and 'United Kingdom' (for Northern Ireland). Links to more websites with Irish MI transcriptions are at Genealogy Links http**://genealogylinks.net/uk/ireland/allireland/cemeteries.htm**.

The subscription-based Irish Family Research (IFR) site has a *Memorials of the Dead* database covering the period from the 1500s up to 1910. The MI transcriptions in the database were made in the late 19th and early 20th century by members of the Association for the Preservation of Memorials of the Dead in Ireland, which was founded in 1888. At the IFR website **www.irishfamilyresearch.co.uk/MEMS.HTM**, you can find lists of all the graveyards included on a county-by-county basis. All counties are included in the database, but the counties with the best coverage are Antrim (51 graveyards), Clare (58), Cork (132), Dublin (101), Kildare (80), Kilkenny (61), Meath (70), Tipperary (66) and Wicklow (46).

You'll also find two volumes (Vol. 2 Part 1 and Vol. 6 Part 1) of the *Journal of the Association for the Preservation of Memorials of the Dead in Ireland* at the Internet Archive **www.archive.org**, which you can view and download free of charge.

The Glasnevin Trust is responsible for five cemeteries and two crematoria in Dublin. You can search the trust's records at **www.glasnevintrust.ie/genealogy**, with full MI details available on a pay-per-view basis.

Many of Belfast's burial records from 1869 are searchable at Belfast City Council's free burial records website **www.belfastcity.gov.uk/burialrecords**. As well as the dates of death and burial, the database contains the age and last address of the deceased person.

Between 1966 and 1990, Irish genealogist Brian J. Cantwell transcribed many MIs, particularly in Counties Wexford (with almost 37,000 names) and Wicklow (with over 18,000). A volume of *Memorials of the Dead* (including Wexford, Wicklow, south County Dublin, west Clare and part of County Cork), compiled and edited by his son Ian Cantwell, who has also compiled a volume of *Memorials of the Dead* covering the west of Counties Galway and Mayo (with more than 8,000 names). You can find both of the above volumes online at the subscription website Irish Origins **www.irishorigins.com** and the subscription/pay-per-view website Findmypast Ireland **www.findmypast.ie**, as well as being available on two CDs from Eneclann **www.eneclann.ie**.

MIs have been transcribed by several Irish family history societies (see Chapter 17), including the Genealogical Society of Ireland **www.familyhistory.ie**, which has published five volumes of MIs from Deansgrange Cemetery, Blackrock, County Dublin, and The North of Ireland Family History Society **www.nifhs.org**, which has published MIs from Counties Antrim and Tyrone.

Clare County Library has made available a large number of donated MI transcriptions at **www.clarelibrary.ie/eolas/coclare/genealogy/genealog.htm**, which have been transcribed by the Kilrush Youth Centre, Clare Roots Society and several individuals around the world.

The Ireland Genealogy Project Archives **www.igp-web.com/IGPArchives/index.htm** has made many MI transcriptions available under the heading 'Cemetery Records' for each county. You'll also find a number of photographs of headstones.

The Gravestone Photos site **www.gravestonephotos.com/countries/ireland.php** partially covers six cemeteries and graveyards in County Tyrone. You can order a free copy of a photograph of a gravestone included in the index.

Irish genealogist Dr. Jane Lyons has been transcribing gravestones since 1996 and her From Ireland website **www.from-ireland.net** now (August 2012) contains more than 19,000 gravestone entries. Jane has also photographed more than 6,700 gravestones in County Laois and over 4,500 in neighbouring County Kilkenny.

Monumental inscriptions at the library of the Society of Genealogists

The Society of Genealogists (SoG) holds copies of many MI booklets in its library. These include Volumes 2-10 of the *Journal of the Association for the Preservation of Memorials of the Dead in Ireland* (published between 1892 and 1920), as well as Volumes 11 and parts of Volumes 12 and 13 of its continuation as the *Journal of the Irish Memorials Association* (published between 1921 and 1937). There is an index of the churchyards and buildings covered up to 1908.

The SoG Library also has many MI transcriptions of individual graveyards and churches in the counties shown in the following table. The numbers of graveyards and churches in the major towns are not included in the county numbers.

County or major town	Number of graveyards and churches covered
Antrim	28
Belfast	11
Carrickfergus	8
Cork	49
Derry/Londonderry	23
Donegal	1
Down	186
Banbridge	6
Downpatrick	6
Dublin	33
Dublin City	8
Fermanagh	2
Kerry	35
Kilkenny	7

County or major town	Number of graveyards and churches covered
Limerick	5
Louth	13
Meath	21
Offaly	3
Roscommon	1
Tipperary	2
Tyrone	3
Waterford	3
Westmeath	2
Wicklow	1

Ruined Irish Church Graveyard.

CHAPTER FOURTEEN
More Websites for Irish Family History

As well as the records and other sources covered in the earlier chapters of this book, there are many other online sources that can help you find out more about your Irish ancestors. Unless otherwise stated, these websites are accessible free of charge.

1641 Depositions

At **www.1641.tcd.ie**, Trinity College Dublin has made available online a database of transcripts and images of 8,000 depositions made by Protestant men and women in the aftermath of the 1641 Roman Catholic rebellion.

Ancestry.co.uk

As well as those mentioned in previous chapters, at the subscription website Ancestry.co.uk **www.ancestry.co.uk**, you'll find databases for the:

- Royal Irish Constabulary 1816-1921 (whose numbers were filled in the early 20th century with many men from England, Scotland, Wales and the United States);
- Lawrence Collection of about 21,000 photographs of all 32 counties of Ireland taken between 1870 and 1910;

- Papers of the Famine Relief Commission 1844-1847 (which was set up to oversee relief of the Great Famine, which led to the deaths of a million Irishmen and women and the emigration of more than a million more);
- Visitation of Ireland (genealogies of families with coats of arms, published in 1897);
- Return of Owners of Land 1876 ('owners of land of one acre and upwards ... including lessees for terms exceeding 99 years, or with a right of perpetual renewal');
- Irish records index 1500-1920 (indexes records donated to the Public Record Office of Ireland after the 1922 fire, and later microfilmed by the LDS Family History Library in Salt Lake City);
- Irish records extraction database (similar to the Irish records index, this database includes records of births, marriages, deaths, burials, census returns and abstracts of around 1,000 wills).

Archive CD Books Ireland

Archive CD Books Ireland **www.eneclann.ie/acatalog/Archive_CD_Books_ Ireland.htm** publishes on CD rare books from the library of Trinity College Dublin and other Irish archives and libraries (and also continues to sell those CDs produced by the former Archive CD Books of the UK). The books include histories, directories, guide books, statistical surveys, indexes to marriage licence bonds, parish registers, census statistical reports, electoral registers, landowner directories, peerage and landed gentry genealogies, as well as Samuel Lewis's *Topographical Dictionary of Ireland 1837*, Sir Arthur Vicars' *Index to the Prerogative Wills of Ireland 1536-1810*, the *Index to the Act or Grant Books and to Original Wills of the Diocese of Dublin 1634-1858*, and *Indexes of Irish [Diocesan] Wills 1536-1858*.

Ballymoney Ancestry

Ballymoney Borough Council's website **www.ballymoneyancestry.com** has a free database of more than 55,000 records, including hearth rolls, Protestant householders' lists, electoral rolls, 1803 agricultural census, tithe Applotment books, Griffith's Valuation, school and church records.

Bann Valley Genealogy

Family historian Richard Torrens's website at **www.torrens.org.uk/Genealogy/ BannValley** holds transcriptions of the registers and monumental inscriptions of 34 Presbyterian, 17 Church of Ireland (Anglican), five Roman Catholic, two Methodist and two Reformed Presbyterian churches in the valley of the River Bann (which forms most of the boundary between Counties Antrim and Derry/Londonderry). The site also includes transcripts of some hearth money rolls, militia lists and rent rolls. Richard Torrens's site links to family historian Lavonne Bradfield's site at **www.angelfire.com/falcon/bannvalley**, which covers the same area.

CMC Record Project

The CMC (christening, marriage and cemetery) record project site **www.cmcrp.net** holds transcripts of baptism, marriage, death, cemetery/headstone and property records for Counties Clare, Cork, Kerry, Limerick, Mayo, Tipperary, Waterford and Wicklow.

Clare County Library

At **www.clarelibrary.ie/eolas/coclare/genealogy/genealog.htm** are transcriptions (for County Clare) of the 1901 census - by townland within district electoral division (DED), 1855 index to Griffith's Valuation, 1823-1837 index to the Tithe Applotment Books, directories from 1788 to 1893, and many other population lists.

Down County Museum

At **www.downcountymuseum.com**, you can search two databases of convict records: one listing around 400 prisoners who were transported to New South Wales, and the other about 1,300 convicts transported to New South Wales and Van Diemen's Land (now Tasmania). The site has links to 20 other prison sites around the world.

Eneclann

Eneclann **www.eneclann.ie/acatalog/All_Releases_En.html** publishes CD transcriptions of various Irish records, including soldiers' wills, Special Branch files on Sinn Fein and Republican suspects 1899-1921 (also on DVD), Memorials of the Dead, the Irish Genealogical Research Society's journal *The Irish Genealogist* 1937-1993, the former magazine *The Irish Ancestor* 1969-1986, 1831 Tithe Defaulters, Grenham's Irish Surnames (see Select Bibliography), the 1851 Dublin City Census, and an Index of Irish Wills 1484-1858 (see Chapter 6).

Fáilte Romhat

Family historian John Hayes' website Fáilte Romhat (meaning 'welcome') **www.failteromhat.com** includes hearth money rolls for Counties Armagh, Louth,

Monaghan and Sligo; scanned images of Pigot's Provincial Directory of Ireland 1824; various lists for County Cork; and a digitised copy of Arthur Young's book *A Tour in Ireland 1776-1779*.

Family and Local History (County Derry/Londonderry)

At family historian Bill Macafee's site **www.billmacafee.com**, you can view and download indexes to various records covering County Derry/Londonderry as well as north and mid County Antrim. The indexes are for the:

- 1630 Muster rolls
- 1660s Hearth money rolls
- 1740 Protestant householders' returns
- 1766 Religious census
- 1796 Flax-growers' list
- 1803 Agricultural census (north County Antrim)
- 1820s/1830s Tithe Applotment Books
- 1831 census (County Derry/Londonderry) - not the actual census (see Chapter 3)
- 1851 census (County Antrim)
- C.1860 Griffith's Valuation

Family Relatives

The subscription website **www.familyrelatives.com** has a collection of Irish records, including:

- Indexes to Irish diocesan wills 1536-1857 (the five-volume set)
- Index to prerogative wills 1536-1810 (Vicars)
- Irish Genealogical Guide (copies and abstracts of wills 1445-1834)
- Quaker abstracts of Dublin wills
- Alumni Dublinenses 1593-1846 (students, graduates, professors and provosts of Trinity College, Dublin)
- Register of the Royal School, Armagh
- Ireland Topographical Directory
- Return of Owners of Land 1876
- McDonald's Trade Directory 1927
- Irish Names and Surnames
- Medical Register for Ireland
- Irish passenger lists (arrivals at New York 1846-1851)

Fermanagh Gold

At **www.fermanagh-gold.com**, family historian Vynette Sage and others have made available their transcriptions of baptisms, marriages, burials, court records and a vast array of other documents relating to County Fermanagh and its county town, Enniskillen. You can carry out a general search of all the databases and download them to your own computer.

Fianna

The Fianna website **www.rootsweb.ancestry.com/~fianna** has information on records relevant to each Irish county, holds transcriptions of records and has links to many other sites with transcripts of Irish records.

Findmypast Ireland

Among the various records at the subscription/pay-per-view site Findmypast Ireland **www.findmypast.ie**, one of the largest databases is that of Irish prison registers from 1790-1924. These records cover more than three and a half million people in the 26 counties of the Republic of Ireland (although I came across a relative of mine in prison in County Cork who came from what is now Northern Ireland). The website has a list of the 44 prisons with covering dates (mostly beginning in the early to mid-19th century.

One of the site's other major databases holds records from the Petty Sessions (magistrates courts) register books from 1851-1910 for most counties in what is now the Republic of Ireland. By the end of 2012, Findmypast expects the database to contain information on more than ten million cases.

Ireland Genealogy Projects Archives

At the **www.igp-web.com/IGPArchives/index.htm** website, you'll find transcriptions of records including those from cemeteries and churches; census returns and substitutes; court records; directories; headstones; land, military and constabulary records; newspapers; obituaries; photographs; vital (civil registration) records; and wills.

Irish Ancestors

Irish professional genealogist John Grenham's pay-per-view 'Irish Ancestors' pages on the *Irish Times* website **www.irishtimes.com/ancestor** provide a good deal of free information, including a 'surname search' that shows the number and county location of households listed in Griffith's Valuation with a specified surname.

Under 'placenames', you can find out the names of all townlands (administrative sub-divisions) in a parish, where the parish is located in its county, names of neighbouring parishes, and the ten most common surnames in the parish (according to Griffith's Valuation). Clicking on 'sitemap', you can find maps showing the Roman Catholic and civil parishes in a county, lists of resources (online and offline) by county, and links to passenger lists and Irish genealogical and historical societies.

Irish Roots magazine

Irish Roots has been published since 1992, and is the only magazine devoted solely to Irish family history. At **www.irishrootsmedia.com**, you can view the latest 32-page issue online, subscribe to either the print or electronic version of the magazine, and buy back copies from 2008 onwards. To purchase previous issues prior to 2008, you need to go to **http://irishroots.ie**.

Library Ireland

The Library Ireland site **www.libraryireland.com** has transcriptions of many old books on Ireland, such as *Irish Names and Surnames*, *Irish Pedigrees*, *A Concise History of Ireland*, *A Compendium of Irish Biography* and *Atlas and Cyclopedia of Ireland*.

You'll also find various interesting articles, such as 'Census of Ireland: 1821, 1831 and 1841 Compared' (from the *Dublin University Magazine*, Volume 23, Number 137, May 1844) and 'Witchcraft in Carrickfergus, County Antrim' (from the *Dublin Penny Journal*, Volume 1, Number 47, 18 May 1833), recounting the last witchcraft trial in Ireland, which took place in 1711.

Ulster Ancestry

In the 'free pages' of the Ulster Ancestry website **www.ulsterancestry.com/ua-free-pages.php**, there are transcriptions of many different types of record, covering Counties Antrim, Armagh, Derry/Londonderry, Donegal, Down, Fermanagh and Tyrone. The free pages also include many ships' passenger lists, mainly of those bound for the USA.

Waterford County Library

At the library's family history page **www.waterfordcountylibrary.ie/familyhistory**, you can view database transcriptions of records for the county. These include death records from 1 January 1864 to 31 December 1901, Griffith's Valuation, extracts from trade directories, Dungarvan Town maps, graveyard inscriptions and graveyard photographs.

Links to other Irish genealogy websites

You'll find links to many other Irish genealogy websites at the following 'portal' sites:

- Cyndi's List **www.cyndislist.com/uk/irl**
- Ireland GenWeb **www.irelandgenweb.com** (with links to county GenWeb sites)
- Northern Ireland GenWeb **https://sites.google.com/site/northernireland worldgenweb** (with links to county GenWeb sites)
- Census Finder **www.censusfinder.com/ireland.htm**
- Census Online **www.census-online.com/links/Ireland**
- The Irish Ancestral Research Association (TIARA) **www.tiara.ie**
- Genealogy Links **http://genealogylinks.net/uk/ireland/index.html**

In addition, there are many Irish links at these United Kingdom portals:

- GENUKI **www.genuki.org.uk/big/irl**
- UKIsearch **www.ukisearch.com/ireland.html**
- UKBMD (births, marriages, deaths and censuses) **www.ukbmd.org.uk**
- UKGDL (genealogical directories and lists) **www.ukgdl.org.uk**
- UKMFH (military family history) **www.ukmfh.org.uk**

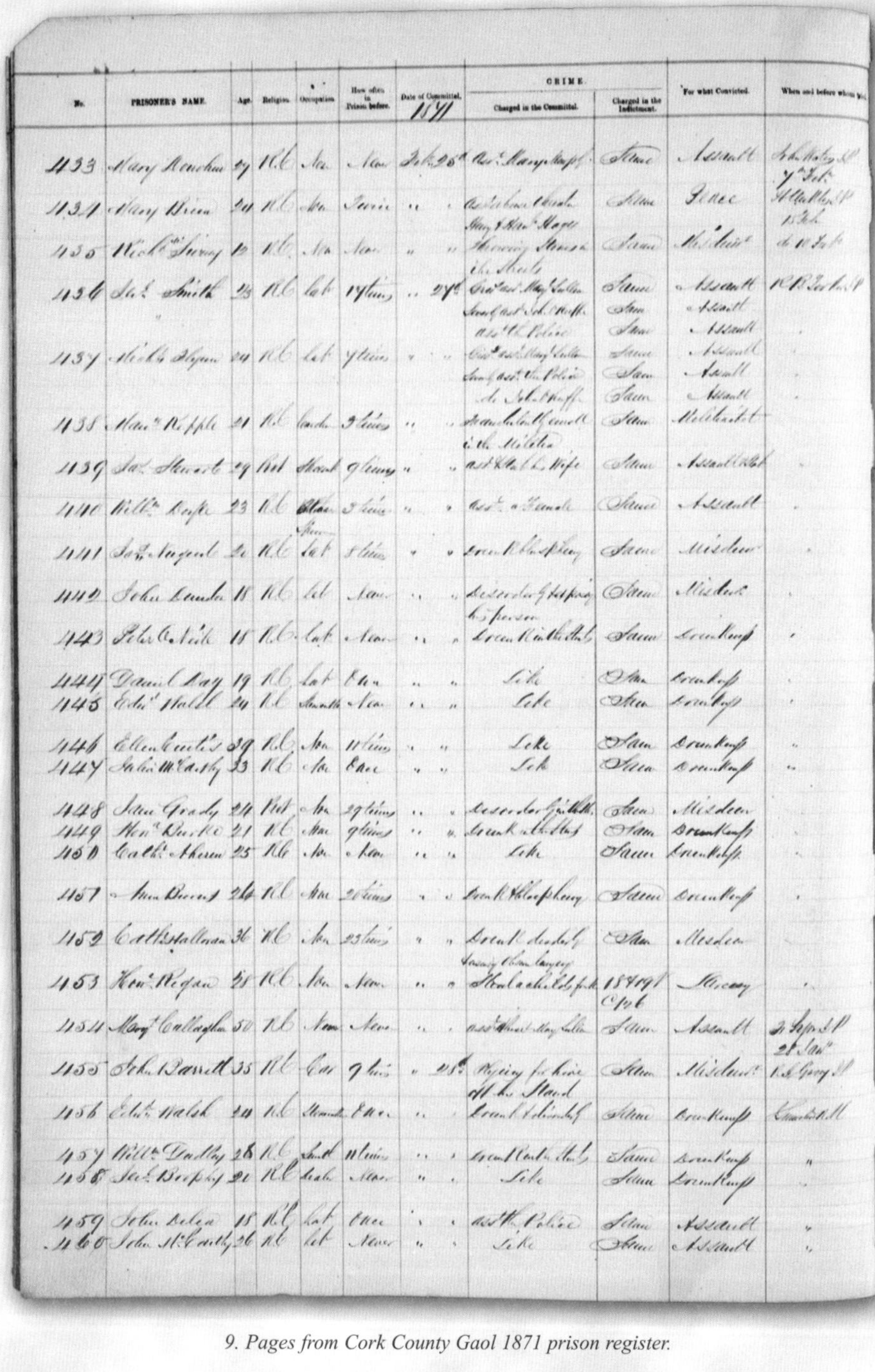

No.	Prisoner's Name	Age	Religion	Occupation	How often in Prison before	Date of Committal 1871	Crime: Charged in the Committal	Crime: Charged in the Indictment	For what Convicted	When and before whom tried
433	Mary [illegible]	47	RC	None	None	Feb 25th	[illegible]	Same	Assault	[illegible] 7th Feb.
434	Mary Brien	24	RC	None	[illegible]	"	[illegible]	Same	Peace	[illegible] 15th
435	Nich[illegible] [illegible]	12	RC	None	None	"	Throwing Stones in the Streets	Same	Misdem[illegible]	[illegible]
436	Jas. Smith	43	RC	Lab	17 times	" 27th	[illegible]	Same	Assault	[illegible]
"							[illegible]	Same	Assault	
							Asst. the Police	Same	Assault	
437	[illegible]	24	RC	Lab	7 times	"	[illegible]	Same	Assault	
							[illegible] asst. the Police	Same	Assault	
							[illegible]	Same	Assault	
438	[illegible]	21	RC	[illegible]	3 times	"	[illegible] the Militia	Same	Misdemeanr.	
439	Jas. Stewart	29	Prot	[illegible]	9 times	"	Asst. & [illegible] Wife	Same	Assault [illegible]	
440	Willm. [illegible]	23	RC	[illegible]	3 times	"	Asst. a Female	Same	Assault	.
441	Jas. Nugent	2[illegible]	RC	Lab	5 times	"	Drunk & blasphemy	Same	Misdem[illegible]	.
442	John [illegible]	18	RC	Lab	None	"	Disorderly & [illegible] his person	Same	Misdem[illegible]	.
443	Peter O'Neill	18	RC	Lab	None	"	Drunk [illegible]	Same	Drunkenness	.
444	Daniel Day	19	RC	Lab	Once	"	Like	Same	Drunkenness	.
445	Edwd. Walsh	24	RC	[illegible]	None	"	Like	Same	Drunkenness	.
446	Ellen [illegible]	39	RC	None	11 times	"	Like	Same	Drunkenness	"
447	Julia McCarthy	23	RC	None	Once	"	Like	Same	Drunkenness	"
448	Jane Grady	24	Prot	None	29 times	"	Disorderly [illegible]	Same	Misdem[illegible]	
449	Hon. Burke	21	RC	None	9 times	"	Drunk [illegible]	Same	Drunkenness	
450	Cathe. Ahern	25	RC	None	None	"	Like	Same	Drunkenness	
451	[illegible] Brien	24	RC	None	20 times	"	Drunk & blasphemy	Same	Drunkenness	
452	Cathe. Halloran	36	RC	None	23 times	"	Drunk disorderly [illegible]	Same	Misdem[illegible]	
453	Hon. Regan	58	RC	None	None	"	[illegible]	1849[illegible] [illegible]	Larceny	
454	Mary Callaghan	50	RC	None	None	"	Asst. [illegible]	Same	Assault	[illegible] 28th Jan.
455	John Barrett	35	RC	Car	9 times	" 28th	[illegible] for hire off his Stand	Same	Misdemeanr.	[illegible]
456	Edwd. Walsh	24	RC	[illegible]	Once	"	Drunk [illegible]	Same	Drunkenness	[illegible]
457	Willm. Dudley	28	RC	Smith	11 times	"	Drunk [illegible]	Same	Drunkenness	"
458	Jas. Brophy	21	RC	[illegible]	None	"	Like	Same	Drunkenness	
459	John Daly	18	RC	Lab	Once	"	Asst. the Police	Same	Assault	"
460	John McCarthy	26	RC	Lab	None	"	Like	Same	Assault	"

9. *Pages from Cork County Gaol 1871 prison register.*

VERDICT.	SENTENCE.	Was it Commuted, and how.	Could Prisoner Read and Write English or Irish when Committed.	Was Prisoner instructed in learning in the Prison, and how far.	Was Prisoner employed in the Prison, and at what.	What was Prisoner's conduct in confinement, and did he or she leave the Prison improved or otherwise.	How long was Prisoner confined. Before Trial. After Trial.	How was Prisoner disposed of.
	Fined 5/- & costs &c Imp 1 Week		No	No	Making	Orderly	7 days	Discharged 3d Novr 1874
	Bound over &c Imp 14 days		No	No	"	"	14 days	Discharged 9th April
	Fined 5/- & costs &c & Imp 48 Hours		Yes	No	"	"	48 hrs	Discharged 27th Feby
	Impd 6 Cal Mos Hd L " 2 Cal Mos Hd Lab		Yes	No	"	"	10 cal mos	Discharged 20th Sept
	Impd 6 Cal Mos Hd L " 2 Cal Mos Hd L &c		Yes	No	"	"	10 cal mos	Discharged 20th Sept
	Fined 5/- & costs &c Imp 3 Cal Month		Yes	No	Platting &c		11 days	Discharged 20th May
	Impd 1 Cal Month & Bd O 1 Cal Mo after		Yes	No	Platting		11 days	Discharged 5th Sept
	Impd 14 days at Hard Labour		Yes	No	Whiting	"	14 days	Discharged 12th March
	Impd 14 days at Hard Labour		Yes	No		"	14 days	Discharged 12th March
	Fined 5/- & costs &c Imp 1 Week		Yes	No	Platting	"	7 days	Discharged 5th March
	Fined 5/- & costs &c Imp 48 Hours		Yes	No	"	"	48 hrs	Discharged 1st March
	Fined 5/- & costs &c Imp 24 Hours		Yes	No	"	"	24 hrs	Discharged 28th Feb
	Fined 5/- & costs &c Imp 24 Hours		No	No	"	"	24 hrs	Discharged 28th Feb
	Fined 5/- & costs &c Imp 48 Hours each		Yes Yes No	No No No	" " "	" "	48 hrs 48 hrs 48 hrs	Discharged
	Imprisoned 1 Week		No	No	"	"	7 days	Discharged 5th March
	Impd 14 days Hard Labour		No	No	Making	"	14 days	Discharged 12th March
	Imprisoned 14 days		No	No	"	"	14 days	Discharged 12th March
	Fined 5/- & costs &c Imp 1 Week		Yes	No	"	"	7 days	Discharged 5th March
	Fined 5/- & costs &c Imp 24 Hours		No	No	"	"	24 hrs	Discharged 1st March
	Fined 5/- & costs &c Imp 48 Hours		Yes	No	"	"	24 hrs	Discharged 2d March
	Fined 5/- & costs &c Imp 24 Hours		Yes	No	"	"	24 hrs	Discharged 1st March
	Impd 14 days Hard Labour		Yes Yes	No	Whiting	"	14 days 14 days	Discharged 13th March

91

CHAPTER FIFTEEN
Irish Resources in the SoG Library

T he library of the Society of Genealogists holds many resources for Irish family history, including transcriptions and indexes in microform and book format. In addition, the society provides Internet access at no charge to several commercial websites and, of course, to all the free sites mentioned in this book.

Although some of the books in the society's library are available online in digitised form, not everyone has Internet access at home, and many of us prefer to use a printed copy of a book if we can.

You'll find the SoG's Irish resources listed in the society's booklet *Sources for Irish Genealogy in the Library of the Society of Genealogists (Library Sources Number 4)*, compiled by Anthony J. Camp (2nd edition, 1998).

In addition, you can find a review of Irish resources in the library on the SoG website at **www.sog.org.uk/prc/irl.shtml**, which gives a general review of resources for the whole of Ireland, as well as those covering 19 of the 32 historic counties. The page lists the parishes and other places on which the society has material.

For detailed up-to-date information on SoG holdings, you need to search the society's online catalogue SOGCAT at **http://62.32.98.6/S10312UKStaff/OPAC**, which shows that the society holds (in January 2012) 3,026 items on Ireland, including 247 microfilms, 156 sets of microfiche and 73 CDs.

Upper Library

Material on the Irish (IR) shelves in the society's Upper Library is grouped in the following categories:

IR/G	General
IR/L	Local
IR/R	Registers
IR/M	Monumental inscriptions
IR/C	Censuses
IR/D	Directories
IR/P	Poll books
IR/PER	Periodicals

The 'general' category includes army, bibliography, biography, deeds and manuscripts, emigration, heraldry, history, Huguenots, newspapers, officials, pedigrees, Presbyterians, 'Quakers', research, surnames and wills.

In its 'periodical' category, the library holds complete runs of *The Irish Ancestor* from its first issue in 1969 up to its last in 1986, *The Irish Genealogist* from its first issue in 1937 to date, *North Irish Roots* from its first issue in 1984 to date, and an incomplete run of the *Journal of the Royal Society of Antiquaries of Ireland* from 1890-1931.

The SoG has copies of all 40 volumes of the *Ordnance Survey Memoirs of Ireland*, as well as copies of *The Civil Survey 1654-1656* and *A Census of Ireland circa 1659*, both published by the Irish Manuscript Commission. You'll also find census fragments, Irish marriage licences, and many will indexes, abstracts and copies in the library, which also holds information on Irish clergymen in around 20 publications (about half of which are included in the 'local' category).

Also in the library are many lists and directories with all-Ireland coverage and dating from 1738 to the late 20th century, as well as a number of county-based directories (including many covering Dublin from 1660-1974, Cork from 1758-1921 and Belfast from 1740-1989).

In the 1940s, Captain George S. Cary compiled over 80 lists of Irishmen and -women who lived between the 17th and 19th centuries, extracting their names from books and manuscripts. Cary's lists, which are held by the SoG, include the names of apprentices, bailiffs, church wardens, clergymen, coroners, high sheriffs, householders, landowners, magistrates, mayors, militia, notaries public, volunteer officers and yeomanry officers. The lists also include marriage and obituary notices, extracted from parish registers and newspapers, and have a surname index.

For researching 'noble' or 'gentry' families, the SoG holds Burke's *Landed Gentry of Ireland* (1898/1899, 1904, 1912 and 1958), Burke's *Irish Family Records* (1976), O'Hart's *Irish Pedigrees* (1892), Howard & Crisp's *Visitation of Ireland* (1897-1918), Lodge's *Peerage of Ireland* (1789), O'Brian's *Corpus Genealogiarum Hiberniae* (1962) and McAnlis's *Consolidated Index to the Records of the Genealogical Office* (1994).

Lower Library

On the society's web page **www.sog.org.uk/library/surnames_and_families.shtml**, you'll find surname indexes to the Surname Document Collection, pedigrees and birth briefs. The Surname Document Collection consists of original documents and transcriptions, such as civil registration birth, marriage and death certificates, parish register entries, wills, deeds, family trees and research notes.

The SoG has a very large collection of family trees, most of which are in the form of roll pedigrees. The society's birth brief collection contains around 28,000 surnames taken from members' birth brief forms, which show a member's ancestry back four generations to his or her great-great-grandparents.

The Lower Library is where you'll find the society's computers, with free Internet access to Ancestry.co.uk, Findmypast, the Origins Network and Family Relatives (which all have transcriptions of many Irish records), as well as to The National Archives' Documents Online (which has many records of Irishmen and -women in its armed forces' collections).

The society also has various CDs (such as those published by Eneclann), microfiche and microfilms, including a number of Roman Catholic parish registers, some census returns - for parts of County Cavan in 1821 and 1841, and for County Derry/Londonderry in 1831(/1834) - and Betham's genealogical abstracts from wills proved in the Prerogative Court of Armagh.

Howth and Ireland's Eye, Co. Dublin, Ireland.

96

CHAPTER SIXTEEN
Irish Archives

Reflecting the division of Ireland between the Republic of Ireland and Northern Ireland, the main archives are situated in both Dublin and Belfast. Both cities have a General Register Office (GRO) and a Public Record Office (PRO), although the PRO in Dublin has been the National Archives of Ireland (NAI) since it was combined with the State Paper Office in 1988.

Dublin also has the Representative Church Body Library and the National Library of Ireland (NLI), which in Autumn 2011 was suggested for merger with the NAI. Some commentators reacted in horror, although a combined national library and public record office seems to work well in Wales (the National Library of Wales in Aberystwyth). In Scotland, the National Archives and GRO are being combined as the National Records of Scotland, although the National Library of Scotland remains independent.

Luckily for those of us who don't live in Ireland, many of the records held in the main Irish archives are available (or can be ordered) online.

General Register Office (GRO) - Irish Republic

The GRO for the Republic of Ireland is based in County Roscommon, but has a research room in Dublin. The Republic's GRO holds civil registration

birth, marriage and death records for all Ireland from 1 January 1864 to 31 December 1921 (and non-Roman Catholic marriages from 1 April 1845) and for the Irish Free State/Republic from 1 January 1922 onwards.

You can download forms from the GRO's website **www.groireland.ie** to order certificates (or cheaper photocopies of them) by post, or you can order them online from the Health Service Executive site **www.hse.ie/eng/services/find_a_service/ bdm/certificates_ie**.

The civil registration indexes are online at both the free website FamilySearch **https://www.familysearch.org** and the subscription-based Ancestry.co.uk **www.ancestry.co.uk** (for all Ireland up to the end of 1921 and the Irish Republic from 1922 onwards), but see my note in Chapter 2 about online ordering.

General Register Office (GRO) - Northern Ireland

The Belfast GRO holds birth and death records for what is now Northern Ireland from 1 January 1864 onwards, but marriage records only from 1 January 1922. Earlier marriages for the area are held by the Irish Republic's GRO and the District Registrar Offices in Northern Ireland.

At the GRO's website **www.nidirect.gov.uk/gro**, you can either download forms to order certificates by post or else order them online (but see my note in Chapter 2). The civil registration indexes at FamilySearch and Ancestry.co.uk cover the counties that are now Northern Ireland only up to the end of 1921.

Northern Ireland's GRO intends to digitise and index its civil registration records and make births over 100 years old, marriages over 75 years old and deaths over 50 years old available online. It hopes to do this by 2013.

National Archives of Ireland (NAI)

The NAI holds the 1901 and 1911 census returns for all Ireland (online at **www.census.nationalarchives.ie**), fragments of some of the earlier censuses, Griffith's Valuation (online at **www.askaboutireland.ie/griffith-valuation**), the Tithe Applotment Books (indexed at **www.ancestry.co.uk**) and records of transportation to Australia in the 19th century (online at **www.nationalarchives.ie/ genealogy/transportation.html**).

There is also an online list of Church of Ireland parish registers held by the NAI. In addition, you'll find at the NAI many other records and documents that are useful for family history research, such as private estate records (many of which are listed online), as well as electoral, education and Poor Law records.

An index of pre-1858 wills, administrations and marriage licences that still exist at the NAI in the form of transcripts, abstracts, extracts, full copies and some original wills is online at both Irish Origins **www.irishorigins.com** and Findmypast Ireland **www.findmypast.ie**. The NAI has also made calendars of wills and administrations from 1923-1982 available online (see Chapter 6).

Public Record Office of Northern Ireland (PRONI)

At the PRONI website **www.proni.gov.uk**, you can search the Ulster Covenant (signed by nearly half a million people in 1912); pre-1840 freeholders' records (of men entitled to vote); nearly 30 digitised street directories from 1819-1900; will calendars for the District Probate Registries of Armagh, Belfast and Londonderry from 1858-1943 (with images from 1858-1900); and a 'Name Search' of pre-1858 wills and administrations, fragments of the 1740 and 1766 religious censuses, 1775 dissenters' petitions, and pre-1920 coroners' inquests. You can also view the Derry/Londonderry Corporation Minute Books 1673-1901 and Register of Freemen 1675-1945.

The site also contains a searchable online catalogue, online guides and indexes (including guides to all church records and newspapers held by the PRONI), and online information leaflets (28 in the PRONI's 'Your Family Tree' series, 10 in its Local History series, three in its Emigration series, five in its Historical Topics series and seven other topics).

National Library of Ireland (NLI)

The NLI **www.nli.ie** holds copies of registers for most Roman Catholic parishes in Ireland and has made available online lists of the parishes covered (alphabetically by diocese), including those in Northern Ireland. Some of these records (particularly for Counties Meath and Roscommon) are indexed at **www.ancestry.co.uk**.

In addition, the NLI holds copies of Griffith's Valuation and the Tithe Applotment Books and has made available family history information leaflets on 'Getting Started', parish registers, valuation records, local studies sources in the NLI and a select bibliography of Irish genealogy and heraldry.

The Chief Herald of Ireland (formerly the Ulster King of Arms) grants and confirms coats of arms to individuals and to organisations. The Office of the Chief Herald (the

Genealogical Office) is a branch of the NLI, at whose website you can view and download a Consolidated Index to the Records of the Genealogical Office compiled by Virginia Wade McAnlis in 1994.

The NLI has set up an online database for Irish research entitled Sources **http://sources.nli.ie**, which contains more than 180,000 catalogue records for Irish manuscripts (both in the NLI and in other libraries and archives) and articles in over 150 Irish periodicals.

Representative Church Body Library (RCBL)

The RCBL holds most of the original copies of surviving Church of Ireland registers of parishes in the Republic of Ireland. The RCBL website **http://ireland. anglican.org/about/42** contains guides to all registers held (with covering dates for baptisms, marriages and burials), as well as to all vestry minute books held (also with covering dates). Many parishes in Northern Ireland are included in these lists. In addition, the RCBL has published parts of the registers and vestry records of a number of parishes.

CHAPTER SEVENTEEN
Irish Family History Societies

Family history societies are always useful, even if you won't be able to go in person to the talks and events that they organise. Societies usually publish a journal with helpful articles on researching in the area that they cover (and on family history in general), while some publish books, booklets and CDs.

All the organisations mentioned below have free websites with information about the societies and their aims, and in some cases they've made available free transcriptions of parish registers, monumental inscriptions, census strays and members' interests.

Council of Irish Genealogical Organisations (CIGO)

CIGO was founded in 1992 as the umbrella organisation for Irish family history, with 13 member societies in Ireland, and 21 overseas. The website **www.cigo.ie** (with many useful weblinks) describes the council's various successful campaigns:

*   the addition of date of birth and parents' names to Irish Republic death certificates;
*   similar proposals added to an official report on Northern Ireland civil registration;

- playing a key role in the release of information from the 1939 National Register;
- the adoption by Fine Gael, the current (January 2012) ruling party in the Republic of Ireland, of a proposal to release the 1926 Irish Free State census in the near future.

Genealogical Society of Ireland (GSI)

Founded in 1990, the GSI holds monthly talks and has a research centre in Dún Laoghaire, near Dublin. The society publishes a monthly Gazette, copies of which (from April 2006 onward) you can read at the GSI website **www.familyhistory.ie**. In addition, you can read the newsletters of the Irish DNA Atlas project launched in November 2011 by the GSI and the Royal College of Surgeons in Ireland.

The society has published several volumes of memorial inscriptions, as well as school registers, census indexes, other population listings and histories of various areas, and is currently developing an online digital archive and library for GSI members and others.

Irish Family History Society (IFHS)

The society was founded in 1984, holds meetings and an annual seminar in Dublin, publishes an annual journal and has a reference library for members. At the IFHS website **www.ifhs.ie**, you can read reviews of family history-related books, magazines and CDs.

Irish Genealogical Research Society (IGRS)

The IGRS was founded in London in 1936 as a learned society by Father Wallace Clare and a number of other people who were concerned about the loss of records in the explosion and fire in the Public Record Office of Ireland in 1922. The core society's reference library includes transcripts of wills and parish registers, and indexes of pedigrees and Irish provincial newspapers. The IGRS also has an Irish branch, which holds seminars and talks in Dublin.

Annually, the society publishes a scholarly magazine called *The Irish Genealogist*, the issues of which from 1937-1993 are available on CD. At the IGRS website **www.igrsoc.org**, you can find listings of the magazine's contents from 1937-2011, and also purchase articles on nine landed families.

Members of the society can download a copy of newspaper indexes (mainly relating to Northern Ireland), as well as early volumes of the IGRS Newsletter (from 1982).

Clare Roots Society (CRS)

Founded in 2006, the CRS holds monthly meetings in Ennis, the county town of Clare. The society has transcribed monumental inscriptions, parish registers (some transcribed by the Clare Roots Diaspora Group in Australia) and memorial cards, as well as other records and publications.

At the CRS website **www.clareroots.org**, you'll find links to society members' websites and other County Clare-related sites. In addition, you can buy the society's publications, including a DVD of a genealogy conference held by the CRS in October 2011 with talks by professional genealogists Nick Barratt and John Grenham (you can see photographs of the conference on the CRS website).

At the free Clare County Library website **www.clarelibrary.ie/eolas/coclare/ genealogy/genealog.htm**, you can view the society's transcriptions of many of the county's graveyards, some parish records and the memorial cards. The CRS transcriptions of 19th century marriages (from 1837) and baptisms (from 1841) in the parish of Ennis are searchable online at the free Ennis Parish website **www.ennisparish.com/genealogy**.

Cork Genealogical Society (CGS)

The CGS was founded in 1994, with more than 50 people attending the first of the society's monthly meetings. The society publishes an annual journal, whose contents are listed on the CGS website **www.corkgenealogicalsociety.com**.

The site has many links to other sites that are useful for County Cork research, such as Margaret Grogan's Cork Pages (with further weblinks) at **http://freepages.genealogy.rootsweb.ancestry.com/~mturner/cork/ire.cork.htm**, which are particularly helpful.

Another link is to the genealogy part of Cork Libraries' Cork Past and Present website **www.corkpastandpresent.ie/genealogy**, which contains 'Contemporary Biographies' of eminent Cork citizens in the early 20th century, complete with photographs.

The Cork Past and Present site also has indexes for the Counties Cork and Kerry material in Albert Casey's 13-volume collection of family history material entitled *O'Kief, Coshe Mang, Slieve Lougher and Upper Blackwater* (covering an area in north-west Cork and eastern Kerry).

North of Ireland Family History Society (NIFHS)

Founded as a family history group in Bangor in 1979, the NIFHS now consists of 12 branches throughout Northern Ireland, all of which have monthly meetings. The society has published a number of booklets and CDs of monumental inscriptions and birth, marriage and death notices from newspapers, and issues a journal twice a year (an index is on the society's website **www.nifhs.org).**

The NIFHS research centre is in Belfast (staffed by volunteers), with a library catalogue that you can download from the website. The society will carry out look-ups in its transcriptions of parish registers and monumental inscriptions (listed on the website) for members who aren't able to visit the research centre.

The society website contains a list of Members' Interests (surnames being researched), tables of over 15,000 'census strays' (Irish people in English censuses), links to many Irish websites (including those of society members) and copies of the NIFHS newsletter.

There are also branch websites for Coleraine **www.coleraine-fhs.org.uk**, Lisburn **http://lisburnfamilyhistory.org.uk** and North Armagh **www.nafhs.org**. The Lisburn site includes three articles, many weblinks and several requests for help. The Coleraine site also has many useful weblinks, while the North Armagh site has a 'bulletin board' for research queries.

Ulster Genealogical and Historical Guild (UGHG)

The UGHG is the membership section of the Ulster Historical Foundation (UHF), which was founded in 1956 and until 1987 formed part of the Public Record Office of Northern Ireland (PRONI).

At the UHF website **www.ancestryireland.com**, anyone can search more than 200 databases (including directories, wills and administrations, as well as occupation, census, education, emigration, election and estate records)**,** but only UGHG members can view the database records. The website also holds an online pay-per-view version of the *History of the Irish Parliament 1682-1800* (also free to UGHG members) with biographies of 2,300 MPs.

The UHF is the county genealogical centre for Counties Antrim and Down, and you can search the indexes to birth/baptism, marriage and death/burial records on a pay-per-view basis. You can do this either at the UHF website (with a discount for UGHG members), at the main Roots Ireland site **www.rootsireland.ie**, at the Antrim

Roots Ireland site **http://antrim.rootsireland.ie** or at the Down Roots Ireland site **http://down.rootsireland.ie**.

The UHF website has civil parish maps for the nine counties of Ulster, lists of the townlands (parish sub-divisions) in each county, and a timeline of Ulster's history and genealogy. In addition, you can download several free e-books from the site, including *My Roots: Tracing Your Belfast Ancestors*.

Western Family History Association (WFHA)

The association was founded in 1995 to cover Counties Clare, Galway, Leitrim, Mayo, Roscommon and Sligo, and holds 5/6 meetings a year in Claregalway, near Galway City. At the association's website **www.wfha.info**, you'll find lists of surnames being researched by members, and of more than a hundred books in the association's library.

SELECT BIBLIOGRAPHY

Many of the books listed are no longer in publication, but you can usually buy copies from a second-hand bookshop or online through Amazon **www.amazon.co.uk** or Abebooks **www.abebooks.co.uk**. In addition, you can find many out-of-copyright Irish books at the Internet Archive **www.archive.org** and at Google Books **http://books.google.co.uk**.

Tracing Irish Ancestry

Tracing Your Irish Ancestors, John Grenham (Gill & Macmillan, 4th edition, 2012) - with around 200 pages listing sources for each county: census returns and substitutes, websites, publications (including local journals and directories), gravestone inscriptions and estate records. Also has 130 pages listing all Roman Catholic parishes and their register coverage, together with county maps of RC parishes.

Trace Your Irish Ancestors, Ian Maxwell (How to Books, 2008).

Your Irish Ancestors: A Guide for Family Historians, Ian Maxwell (Pen & Sword, 2008) - the first of these books concentrates on research, while the second includes detailed social history (about 2/3 of the book).

Researching Scots-Irish Ancestors, William J. Roulston (Ulster Historical Foundation, 2005) - covering sources for research in all nine counties of Ulster in the 17th and 18th centuries, with appendices (about half the book) listing pre-1800 church and estate records, as well as records for individual parishes.

Irish Ancestry: A Beginner's Guide, Bill Davis (Federation of Family History Societies, 3rd edition, 2001) - including a good deal on emigration from Ireland.

Irish Genealogy: A Record Finder, edited by Donal F. Begley (Heraldic Artists, 1981) - including lists of census returns and substitutes, directories, newspapers and the surnames in Matheson's *Special Report* of 1890.

Irish Church Records, edited by James G. Ryan (Flyleaf Press, 2nd edition 2001) - covering Roman Catholic, Church of Ireland, Presbyterian, Methodist, Baptist, 'Quaker', Huguenot and Jewish records.

Irish Family and Local History Handbook, edited by Robert and Elizabeth Blatchford (Robert Blatchford Publishing, 2011) - an Irish version of the popular

Family and Local History Handbook that the Blatchfords have been editing and publishing for over ten years. Very good for addresses and contact details, as well as general articles about Irish family history.

Clans, families and surnames

The Clans of Ireland, John Grenham (Gill & Macmillan, 1993) - the first part of the book covers Irish immigration and emigration, and the rest consists of entries for about 200 families, describing their origins and location and illustrating their coats of arms in full colour.

The Surnames of Ireland, Edward MacLysaght (Irish Academic Press, 6th edition, 1985) - a dictionary of surnames found in Ireland with the origins and history of each name, as well as maps showing where the main families lived in the period after the 12th/13th century Anglo-Norman invasion and before the 17th century. MacLysaght points out that many seemingly English surnames found in Ireland are actually Anglicisations of Gaelic surnames.

Grenham's Irish Surnames, John Grenham (Eneclann, 2003) [CD] - a more detailed version of his Irish Ancestors section of the Irish Times website **www.irishtimes.com/ancestor**. When you enter a surname (there are more than 26,000 to choose from), the CD will show you on a map of Ireland the location of households with that name in the mid-19th century, according to Griffith's Valuation. The software also lists the number of households with the name in each of Ireland's 32 counties.

If you click on a county name (or on the map), then a map of civil parishes is displayed with a breakdown of households with the name in each parish. Clicking on a parish name will give you information on the records of the various religious denominations in that parish, including their locations. The CD also holds surname histories and coats of arms.

Other useful publications about Ireland

The Irish in Britain, John Archer Jackson (Routledge and Kegan Paul, 1963) - covering Irish migration to Britain in the 19th and 20th centuries, with maps showing the percentage of Irish-born people in Britain by county in the 1841, 1861, 1891 and 1951 censuses, and a table giving the numbers migrating from Ireland to Britain each year from 1876-1920.

Atlas of Irish History, general editor Seán Duffy (Gill & Macmillan, 2nd edition, 2000) - with about 50 maps of Ireland's history from the time of the Celtic-speaking peoples of about 100 AD, through the Viking Wars (in the 9th century), English invasion (12th century), English and Scottish 'Plantations' (16th and 17th centuries), 1641 Rising, 1798 Rebellion, the Great Famine (the late 1840s), the decline of the Gaelic language, the Easter Rising (1916), Anglo-Irish War (1919-21) and the partition of Ireland (1922), to the 'Troubles' in Northern Ireland (late 20th century).

The Oxford Companion to Irish History, edited by S.J Connolly (Oxford University Press, 1998) - more than 1,800 A-Z entries in around 600 pages, covering everything from Brian Boru (King of Munster in the late 10th century) to seasonal migration (between 60,000-100,000 a year in the mid-19th century).

A History of Ulster, Jonathan Bardon (The Blackstaff Press, 1992) - more than 800 pages on Ulster's history from 7000BC to 1992 in 15 chapters, including the 16th century Elizabethan conquest, 17th century plantation and 20th century partition.

The People of Ireland, edited by Patrick Loughrey (Appletree Press/BBC Northern Ireland) - 11 chapters on the peoples who make up the Irish today, including the earliest immigrants, Celts, Vikings, Normans, English and Scots.

INDEX

About the SOCIETY OF GENEALOGISTS

Founded in 1911 the Society of Genealogists (SoG) is Britain's premier family history organisation. The Society maintains a splendid genealogical library and education centre in Clerkenwell.

The Society's collections are particularly valuable for research before the start of civil registration of births marriages and deaths in 1837 but there is plenty for the beginner too. Anyone starting their family history can use the online census indexes or look for entries in birth, death and marriage online indexes in the free open community access area.

The Library contains Britain's largest collection of parish register copies, indexes and transcripts and many nonconformist registers. Most cover the period from the sixteenth century to 1837. Along with registers, the library holds local histories, copies of churchyard gravestone inscriptions, poll books, trade directories, census indexes and a wealth of information about the parishes where our ancestors lived.

Unique indexes include Boyd's Marriage Index with more than 7 million names compiled from 4300 churches between 1538-1837 and the Bernau Index with references to 4.5 million names in Chancery and other court proceedings. Also available are indexes of wills and marriage licences, and of apprentices and masters (1710-1774). Over the years the Society has rescued and made available records discarded by government departments and institutions but of great interest to family historians. These include records from the Bank of England, Trinity House and information on teachers and civil servants.

Boyd's and other unique databases are published on line on **www.findmypast.com** and on the Society's own website **www.sog.org.uk**. There is free access to these and many other genealogical sites within the Library's Internet suite.

The Society is the ideal place to discover if a family history has already been researched with its huge collection of unique manuscript notes, extensive collections of past research and printed and unpublished family histories. If you expect to be carrying out family history research in the British Isles then membership is very worthwhile although non-members can use the library for a small search fee.

The Society of Genealogists is an educational charity. It holds study days, lectures, tutorials and evening classes and speakers from the Society regularly speak to groups around the country. The SoG runs workshops demonstrating computer programs of use to family historians. A diary of events and booking forms are available from the Society on 020 7553 3290 or on the website **www.sog.org.uk** .

Members enjoy free access to the Library, certain borrowing rights, free copies of the quarterly *Genealogists' Magazine* and various discounts of publications, courses, postal searches along with free access to data on the members' area of our website.

More details about the Society can be found on its extensive website at **www.sog.org.uk**

For a free Membership Pack contact the Society at:

14 Charterhouse Buildings,
Goswell Road,
London EC1M 7BA.
Telephone: 020 7553 3291
Fax: 020 7250 1800

The Society is always happy to help with enquiries and the following contacts may be of assistance.

Library & shop hours:

Monday	Closed
Tuesday	10am - 6pm
Wednesday	10am - 6pm
Thursday	10am - 8pm
Friday	Closed
Saturday	10am - 6pm
Sunday	Closed

Contacts:

Membership
Tel: 020 7553 3291
Email: membership@sog.org.uk

Lectures & courses
Tel: 020 7553 3290
Email: events@sog.org.uk

Family history advice line
Tel: 020 7490 8911
See website for availability

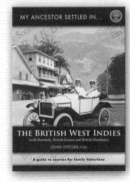

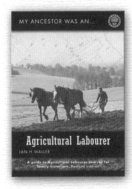

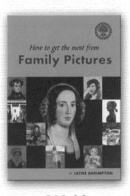